Stadium Stories:
Chicago Bears

Stadium Stories™ Series

Stadium Stories:
Chicago Bears

Lew Freedman

INSIDERS' GUIDE®

GUILFORD, CONNECTICUT
AN IMPRINT OF THE GLOBE PEQUOT PRESS

INSIDERS' GUIDE®

Copyright © 2006 by Morris Book Publishing, LLC

Text design: Casey Shain

Cover photos: *front cover:* Brian Urlacher (Chicago Tribune Archives); *back cover:* top, Bronko Nagurski (George Brace Collection); bottom, Walter Payton (Chicago Tribune Archives)

Library of Congress Cataloging-in-Publication Data

Freedman. Lew.
    Stadium stories : Chicago Bears / Lew Freedman. — 1st ed.
      p. cm. — (Stadium stories series)
    ISBN-13: 978-0-7627-4094-9
    ISBN-10: 0-7627-4094-9
      1. Chicago Bears (Football team)—History. I. Title. II. Series
GV956.C5F735 2006
796.332'640977311—dc22   2006045721

Manufactured in the United States of America
First Edition/First Printing

Contents

Acknowledgments

I was going on ten years old when I began following professional football and collecting trading cards. One of the first great teams I appreciated was the Chicago Bears of 1963, the squad that gave George Halas his last world championship.

Reliving that championship season through research and conversations with some of the participants was an especially enjoyable part of this project. For their help with that chapter and the other golden moments captured in this book, I would like to thank the Chicago Bears organization, especially senior director of corporate communications Scott Hagel; the Pro Football Hall of Fame in Canton, Ohio, and its research library; and the Bears players who cooperated with interviews.

Introduction

The Chicago Bears are the cornerstone franchise of the National Football League, the original building block of the gridiron skyscraper that now towers over America. The Bears were there at the beginning, when professional football was still a fledgling operation. The Bears were forward thinking when college football ruled the sport. And more than eighty-five years later, they remain an essential ingredient in the firmament of the game, in the heartland of the sport's fan base.

The birth of the team and the league was a simultaneous conception. The growth of the team and the league has been a simultaneous evolution. The Bears owe the NFL, and the NFL owes the Bears, and there is no history of the one without the other.

Team and league came together like the confluence of two rivers in the bloodstream of one man, George S. Halas. He was the founder of the Decatur Staleys. He led the southern Illinois team through its difficult beginnings, he renamed it the Chicago Bears, and for decades he served as the crusty, hard-nosed leader of a league inexorably maturing into the most significant and professional team sports organization in the United States.

The Chicago Bears, winners of nine championships, were Halas's brainchild and baby and his legacy. The legendary Halas begat us the legendary Chicago Bears and their offspring—from Red Grange to Bronko Nagurski, from Sid Luckman to George Connor, from Gale Sayers to Walter Payton, from Bill George to Dick Butkus, from Mike Ditka to Brian Urlacher.

There has been joy in memorable championships—in 1963 and the Super Bowl of 1985. There has been laughter—*The*

Super Bowl Shuffle. There have been tears—*Brian's Song* and the premature death of Payton.

Through it all, the Bears have been the Monsters of the Midway, the living embodiment of a hardworking, tough town, ever so proud of its always tough team.

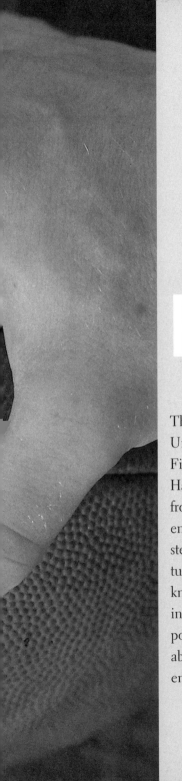

Papa Bear

The set of the jaw told the story of the man. Unflinching. Pugnacious. Determined. Firm. Bold. You could look at George S. Halas's jawline and read his mind. Shown from a certain angle, the jaw seemed large enough to precede him into a room by a full step. The man who gave Chicago the institution of the Chicago Bears was a man who knew what he wanted, was guided by locked-in ideas, knew how to acquire and wield power, and was neither ashamed nor shy about using it to further his and his team's ends. Yet Halas was not blind to the common good, either, and if many of his players thought of him as a cheapskate in contract negotiations, he was, in keeping with his role as godfather of the franchise, a fascinating mix of hard-headed and softhearted.

Gale Sayers, one of the greatest running backs in NFL history, said, "I love George Halas." Mike Ditka, one of the most colorful characters in NFL history, considered Halas such a skinflint he accused him of "throwing nickels around like manhole covers." Yet he also revered "The Old Man."

Halas was born on February 2, 1895, on Chicago's West Side, of Bohemian heritage. His family originated in Pilsen, now part of the Czech Republic, and had to hustle for every dollar by operating a grocery store/saloon. Halas delivered newspapers in the mornings before school and attended Crane Technical High School. He went on to the University of Illinois, where he won varsity letters in football, basketball, and baseball, then joined the navy. Halas briefly played Major League baseball for the New York Yankees, just as Babe Ruth was coming into his own as a slugger after being traded from the Boston Red Sox.

Halas's career lasted twelve games, and he batted .091, a suggestion that his fiery temperament might be better suited to the on-field collisions of football. Halas, who earned a civil engineering degree, accepted a job in March of 1920 working for A. E. Staley's starch factory in Decatur, Illinois, with the stipulation that he create a company football team. Players held jobs at the business, practiced on company time, and got paid extra. Staley used the team—the Decatur Staleys—as an advertising vehicle.

It was a good deal for former collegians who wished to stay in the game. Professional football had operated on the fringes of the

The Original National Football League

During the fall of 1920, the American Professional Football Association, the forerunner of the National Football League, played its first season. The teams that played either a full league season or competed against league teams were as follows:

Decatur Staleys (which in 1922 became the Chicago Bears)
Akron Pros
Buffalo All-Americans
Chicago Racine Cardinals
Rock Island Independents
Dayton Triangles
Rochester Jeffersons
Canton Bulldogs
Detroit Heralds
Cleveland Tigers
Chicago Tigers
Hammond Pros
Columbus Panhandles
Muncie Flyers

The league was densely populated with clubs from Illinois, Ohio, Indiana, and upstate New York. If college football was first prominent in the northeastern part of the United States, professional football has its deepest roots in the fertile soil of the Midwest.

American sports scene for a couple of decades but with limited organization and opportunity. Some entrepreneurs sought to change that.

When a meeting was held September 17, 1920, in the offices of Ralph Hay's Hupmobile auto dealership in Canton, Ohio, to discuss founding a professional league, Halas was present on Staley's behalf. The gathering decided that the ten teams represented would each pay a $100 entry fee and become members of the American Professional Football Association. It was said there were not enough chairs available for the participants, and some of the overflow rested their behinds on the running boards of the cars.

A few weeks later, on October 3, the Decatur Staleys made their debut, defeating the Moline Tractors, 20–0. Halas was twenty-five. In the early days of football, players competed on both offense and defense, and Halas, an end, made his mark on the field with one enduring, spectacular play. Pictures of him at the time show a thick-haired young man with determination in his sleepy eyes but with the optimism of youth seeping through.

In a game against the Oorang Indians at Wrigley Field in Chicago, Halas scooped up a Jim Thorpe fumble and ran it 98 yards for a touchdown. The length of the run was a record and remained so for forty-nine years. Halas later said he knew that Thorpe—who was eventually named the greatest athlete of the first half of the twentieth century—was angry. Halas was motivated to outrun Thorpe to save himself a vicious hit. Halas took off downfield, zigging and zagging. "I knew he was a bit faster," Halas said, "and he would catch me."

It is ironic that attempts to establish professional football in 1920 closely resemble the shift from amateurism in the Olympic

Bears founder, coach, owner, and all-around leader George Halas points out the lineup of the 1921 Decatur Staleys, forerunner of the Bears before they moved to Chicago. *George Brace Collection*

movement decades later. Now, many athletes in so-called minor sports hold jobs through personal sponsorships with companies and train on company time.

The inaugural squad of the Decatur Staleys completed a 10–1–2 season. Although the Staleys had the largest number of wins, the Akron Pros finished unbeaten at 8–0–3. A year later Halas led the Staleys to the first championship in team history. The club finished 9–1–1 and won the title with the best record, even though there was no official championship game. The team suited up eighteen players wearing leather helmets and little padding.

After the season, however, Staley informed Halas that his business could no longer support the team. He turned the club over to Halas and allowed him to move it to Chicago. For a $5,000 payment, he persuaded Halas to keep the nickname Staleys for one additional season.

In January of 1922, the Decatur Staleys became the Chicago Bears. Halas chose the name because he liked the Chicago Cubs baseball team's name. Appropriately, given the size of athletes populating the two sports, Bears were the big brothers of the Cubs. And yes, especially with Halas at the helm, they growled louder.

The move to the Midwest's largest city was the start of a special relationship that linked team and place with mutual respect early on. Halas remained a player until 1929 and spent the next five-and-a-half decades in roles as distinctive as president and coach. Regardless of his title of the moment (and there were interruptions in his coaching tenure, such as when he entered World War II as a navy commander), Halas was always the face of the franchise.

Between 1920 and his death in 1983, Halas turned over coaching duties to others four times. His lifetime mark was 324–151–31, and his record for wins stood for a decade after his death until broken by Don Shula of the Miami Dolphins. Under

Halas's oversight, the Bears won championships in 1921, 1932, 1933, 1940, 1941, 1943, 1946, and 1963. Not straying far from what he knew, Halas bestowed the University of Illinois colors on the Bears uniforms. They have since worn blue, orange, and white. The team's ninth championship was won at the end of the 1985 season—after the founder's death—under the tutelage of Mike Ditka, Halas's handpicked coach.

As a coaching innovator, Halas was appreciated for being the first to use film to study games, and with the collaboration of assistant Clark Shaughnessy, he introduced the T-formation to the pros. He was early to recognize the value of newspaper coverage and through his friendship with local media moguls understood how fruitful a marriage with television would be for the future of the sport. Halas also exercised his will, sometimes behind the scenes, in the selection of key NFL leaders, including Commissioner Bert Bell in the 1950s.

For many years, Halas treated the NFL as a personal fiefdom. As it grew and expanded, he continued to wield influence, but he lost his grip on the daily operations. During the course of his lifetime, however, Halas never surrendered his personal stranglehold on the Bears.

Papa Bear certainly made an early impression on his players. Long after his playing days ended, he prowled the sidelines wearing a trench coat and fedora, barking at officials. Halas took every call personally, and nothing seemed to regulate the flow of insults pouring out of his mouth. He swore regularly at players during practice. And when it came time to negotiate contracts, he was a take-it-or-leave-it boss. Frequently, Halas sought to portray his players as better off than others around the league, but he couldn't the players all of the time. Many realized they were but few took their challenges very far. Many players ...... , and many didn't know what to make of him.

"Halas was simply the National Football League," said 1960s era defensive back Roosevelt Taylor, who is from Louisiana. "I hadn't met many people in my life, and certainly not millionaires from a big city, like him. Everything he did just amused me or amazed me."

Like an authoritarian teacher, Halas did not tolerate much guff or talking back from his players. "It was established when I first got there that not many people went against him," Taylor said. "The things he said to do, or not to do, you did it his way."

Halas later told people that the $100 league-initiation fee was never paid by many of the original league owners. Their ideas were bigger than their wallets. Throughout the early days of the league and throughout the 1930s, when America was pummeled by the Depression, Halas struggled to make payroll, to keep the Bears afloat, and to always build for the future. On occasion he came close to not meeting his obligations, and certainly those difficult times helped form his opinion about just what was a fair salary for even the best of ballplayers despite more prosperous times later.

"He came up the hard way," said Hall of Fame Lineman Stan Jones, who played on Halas's last title team in 1963. "Making payrolls, the Depression. It would have been a little tough. He was a tough guy, but he had a soft core. He was hard on the outside, and he was always afraid a player would ask for money."

Although individual instances were not often publicized at the time, Halas was also renowned for assisting a player in financial trouble or for helping out a player's family. He had money for their emergencies, even if he never seemed to have it for their contracts. Two sides of the same coin—generosity and stinginess. Perhaps both of them stemmed from the same trait. The "Old Man," as his later players referred to Halas, had to be in charge. In every way.

Fullback Rick Casares, an enduring favorite as a Bears player from the 1963 championship team, remembered the animosity between Halas and quarterback George Blanda. Blanda seemed forever doomed to backup status with the Bears, but when he was cut loose and signed with the American Football League, he became pro football's most prolific scorer and had a career that lasted more than twenty years. The spite cut was clearly a Bears personnel mistake.

"Halas sent in a play one time, and I was in the huddle," Casares said. "Blanda said, 'BS, I'm not calling that.' That's Blanda for you. Instead, Blanda threw a swing pass to me, and I scored. Halas couldn't wait for him to get off the field. He was screaming at him. Even though we scored.

"Blanda didn't play any more that game. Blanda was the best kicker in the NFL, but when Halas made Blanda retire, we went into the next season with no place kicker. They were trying out guys that hadn't kicked. Then George went to the Houston Oilers and won a championship and made more money in one year than he did his entire career with the Bears."

That was Papa Bear, the most stubborn man in the Midwest when he wanted to be. Late in his career he also feuded with George Allen. Allen was his most loyal assistant, and he dreamed of taking over the Bears' reins one day. But when it became

Defense from the Start

Throughout their history, the Chicago Bears have been synonymous with defense. Their nickname, "Monsters of the Midway," illustrates the point.

In the first season of the Bears' existence in 1920, when they were known as the Decatur Staleys, the franchise played thirteen games and recorded ten shutouts. That's more zeroes than most Major League pitchers ever see in a row.

Founder George Halas, penurious from the start, fielded a club at the salary cost of $1,900 per man—a bargain. Shutting out ten foes in a season is not something that occurs in the modern-day National Football League. Shutting out one team in the present day is regarded as notable.

apparent that Halas was not about to step down as coach, Allen moved on and became a hated rival.

J. C. Caroline, another University of Illinois alumnus, who played both halfback and defensive back for the Bears between 1956 and 1965, viewed Halas as a challenging but fair coach when it involved performance on the field and very much of a bag of contradictions when it came to matters of the pocket book.

"He let you know what you were doing right and what you were doing wrong," Caroline said while laughing at the thought. "He was kind of a hardnosed coach, but if you did your job, he would take care of you. You know, not pay you a lot of money, but if you had problems—and some guys did have problems during the off-season running into a financial struggle—they could call Halas. Halas would bail them out."

Harlon Hill, who emerged from Florence State Teachers College as a gazellelike wide receiver in 1954, had no fear of George Halas when he advanced to the pros. He didn't know much about him. He didn't know Halas was supposed to be a gruff guy who was tough to play for, who cared for his players but didn't always show it.

"He was a great guy," Hill said. "He loved to play football, and he loved the Bears, and he gave you 100 percent. That's all he asked for from you. He didn't talk to his players personally too much. He would be real close to them, but you couldn't tell that easily if he liked you or not."

Hill was an unlikely rookie starter, so he might assume that Halas liked him. But he saw the other side of Halas across his big desk. "He liked you until you started negotiating contracts," Hill said. "He was just tough that way."

Hill's observation that Halas just loved to play football was an interesting one, since Halas's days as an active player ended before Hill was born. Unlike some franchises, however, which recognize a key contribution from a founder or longtime owner or administrative official, the Bears did not retire number 1 to honor Halas. Rather, his number 7 playing jersey was retired after his death. The last Bear player to wear number 7 was quarterback Bob Avellini in 1984.

Although football players are not known for being squeamish, some of them were startled that an elderly fellow like Halas possessed a nasty vocabulary that eclipsed that of the most foul-mouthed comedian. Halas seemed well armed with a dictionary containing only four-letter words, and during practice and pregame talks he liberally applied them to upcoming opponents. Johnny Lujack, the one-time Notre Dame star quarterback who played for the Bears between 1948 and 1951, once said, "When I was in the service, I never heard such words."

There is little doubt Halas was a complex, layered man, but his life's work and play revolved around the Bears. Late in his coaching career, Halas drafted running back Gale Sayers out of Kansas. They had a special bond, and Sayers said that from the start of his abbreviated career, Halas gave him good advice on how to prepare for a postfootball life. Sayers said that Halas and he had a father-son relationship and called him "just a great man."

If their rapport was indeed that special, there was also room in the family for another son—Mike Ditka. Ditka was an All-American from the University of Pittsburgh who, much like Halas, burned at his core for victory. Admiring Ditka's toughness and grit—perhaps seeing something of himself in the twenty-one-year-old—the sixty-five-year-old Halas transformed Ditka into a pioneer game-breaking tight end. Ditka played a major role on Halas's final championship team in 1963.

Halas gave up coaching for the last time in 1967, but as anyone who shook hands with him could attest, he still ran Bears operations with an iron grip for sixteen more years. Later (and probably inevitably) Halas and Ditka butted heads, and Ditka was exiled to the Dallas Cowboys after the 1966 season. Many years in the future, Ditka wrote a letter to Halas that proved to be

Papa Bear and his wife, Wilhemina "Min" Halas. George Brace Collection

a landmark in team literature. In the letter Ditka, who had experience as an NFL assistant coach, informed Halas that he bled Bears orange and blue and was the right man to restore NFL glory to the team as the next coach of the Bears.

The letter touched a chord. Halas agreed that Ditka was the right man at the right time, and he appointed Ditka coach of the Bears in 1982. Before Halas died of cancer at the age of eighty-eight in 1983, he gave Ditka a bottle of champagne and told him not to open it until he led the Bears to a Super Bowl championship. The mission was fulfilled two years later.

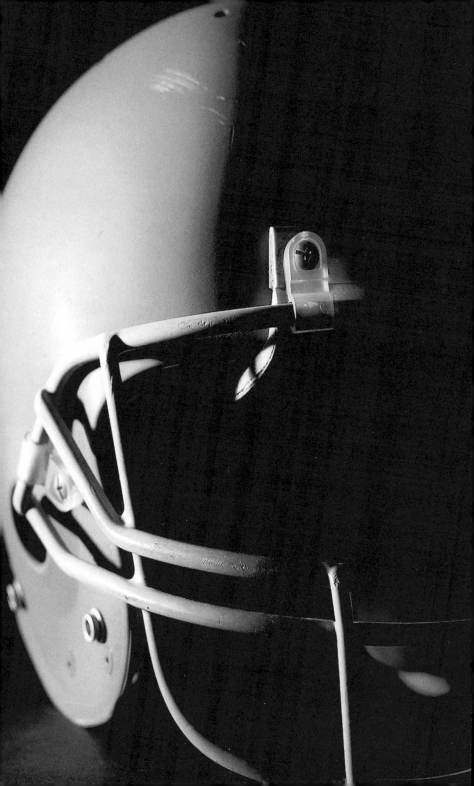

The Galloping Ghost

It just may be the best, most evocative sports nickname of all time: the Galloping Ghost. What better appellation for a running back? Elusive, wisplike, the image of defenders grabbing futilely at the rush of wind where the man passed. Perfect.

Harold "Red" Grange, whose hair inspired that moniker, was the first great star of profes-

Harold "Red" Grange was
professional football's first
superstar.
George Brace Collection

sional football. If George Halas and his fellow operators in that automobile showroom invented the league that gave the sport its true jump start, then Grange became its public face, its initial legend, the standard bearer most clearly identified.

And best of all for Halas, Grange was a Bear. While Halas benefited from Grange's exalted status following a brilliant career at the University of Illinois, he also nurtured Grange's name to mythic stature, to their mutual satisfaction.

Grange was born on June 13, 1903, in Pennsylvania, but after his mother died when he was five, his dad moved to Wheaton, Illinois, about 25 miles west of Chicago, to become the police chief. Coming from a basic, if not needy, background, Grange worked part time delivering ice blocks to his neighbors, and when his feats of athleticism transferred to the gridiron, the nickname bestowed on him was "The Wheaton Iceman." It was catchy but was soon enough overshadowed when his running exploits demanded a more flowery description. The famed sportswriter Grantland Rice was on hand to witness them—more about that later. He stood 6'0" and weighed 180 pounds in an era when that was big enough, and he had a track man's speed, so when Grange was let loose on the ball field by legendary Illinois coach Bob Zuppke, he seemed untouchable to the slower, bulkier defenders. As a three-time All-American, Grange became a national sensation when college football was the big daddy of the game and pro football was a mere scuffling sideshow.

Not many folks were calling Grange "Harold" by the time he established his magnificence with a football in his arms. "Red" did fine for most. And "The Wheaton Iceman" gave the press something to play with. But Grange's special effort against Michigan in 1924 made believers of all doubters, recorded his ability as an irresistible force, and was deserving of a special mention in a fresh pantheon of achievement.

Clearly, you couldn't tackle what you couldn't see, and the Galloping Ghost was as ethereal as any running back in history when he accounted for 6 touchdowns against the Wolverines. Illinois defeated Michigan 39–14 on October 18, 1924, at Memorial Stadium in Champaign, and it might be appropriately written that it was Grange 39, Michigan 14.

In the first quarter, Grange erupted for touchdown runs of 95, 67, 56, and 45 yards. In the second half he scored again on a 64-yard run and then threw a pass for a sixth touchdown. The game made Grange's fame, and by the time Grange finished matriculating in Champaign, the school record book listed 3,637 yards gained and 31 touchdowns next to his name.

Halas drove to Champaign in 1924 in order to see Grange play in person and came away from a game played in the pouring rain anxious to make him a Bear.

"For a year I pondered," Halas wrote in his autobiography. "I wrote Grange a couple of letters but received no reply. I spoke to him on the phone, to no avail."

Grange was never boastful. He once explained his prowess carrying the football very simply. "I played football the only way I knew," said Grange, who lived until the age of eighty-seven. "If you have the football and eleven guys are after you, if you're smart, you'll run. It was no big deal."

Others thought it was. The nation's sports fans fell in love with Grange's dashing ways on the field and his self-effacing demeanor off it. The subject of intense adoration, Grange always

Who Are Those Guys?

Red Grange had the name that glittered most brightly for the Chicago Bears during the 1920s, but the first player who ever signed to play for the Chicago Bears as opposed to the Decatur Staleys was tackle Ed Healey. Halas bought Healey's contract from the Rock Island Independents for $100.

Keeping in mind that entire teams had paid $100 to enter the league only two years before, it might be said that Papa Bear Halas held Healey in high esteem. Healey probably earned back his purchase price with a single play in a 1924 game. A teammate got turned around on an interception and was running the wrong way with the ball. Healey tracked him down after a 30-yard stalk and tackled him to save a touchdown.

Roy "Link" Lyman joined the Bears in 1926 after playing elsewhere. A tackle who reached the Pro Football Hall of Fame, Lyman played no high school football because his school had only seven boys.

Center George Trafton, who was considered the best at his position in the early days of the NFL, played for Knute Rockne at Notre Dame but was kicked off the team when the coach caught him playing semipro ball. Real pro ball, over thirteen seasons for the Bears, was more his style.

Probably the biggest-name player affiliated with Chicago and Halas before Grange was back John "Paddy" Driscoll. Driscoll was a member of the Staleys, played with the Chicago Cardinals, then rejoined the Bears after the 1925 season. Driscoll ran, punted, and drop kicked field goals, certainly a forgotten art today. Driscoll scored 27 points in a game in 1923 and kicked a 50-yard field goal in 1925.

Even though Grange was well aware that he was despised in some quarters for taking money to play ball (he once said, "The only thing I could have done worse was kill somebody. I was called everything possible."), Driscoll was taken to task at home for possibly misconstruing the fans' expressed displeasure.

In the first game of the Red Grange tour, Driscoll reportedly went home and told his wife that it was awful the way the fans booed Grange in the 0–0 tie in which the Galloping Ghost did little of significance. She as much as called Driscoll a bonehead, telling him that the spectators were booing him for not giving Grange the ball often enough.

praised his teammates. Grantland Rice, who gave the Four Horsemen of Notre Dame their nickname, labeled him the Galloping Ghost. Damon Runyon, whose work inspired the Broadway show *Guys and Dolls*, said Grange "on the field is the equal of three football players and a horse." Grange immortalized his number 77 uniform jersey.

Perhaps if Grange did what most of his fellow collegiate stars did at the time—head into the regular workforce following graduation, he would be best recalled these many decades later for his single astonishing performance against Michigan.

However, what Grange did following his last appearance in Illini blue and orange forever stamped him in football consciousness as someone different and special. Grange remembered well his physical efforts carrying ice to raise money to help pay for college. So when an extraordinary offer came his way to turn professional and capitalize on his gridiron name immediately, he had to be thinking, "No more ice for me."

This was the Roaring Twenties, a time when the United States partied over its marvelous financial fortune, when sports stars first gained fame on the order of Hollywood stars. There were six-day bicycle races, flagpole sitters, and dance marathons entertaining the masses. Babe Ruth was elevating baseball. Bobby Jones was the king of the golf world. Big Bill Tilden owned the tennis courts. And Jack Dempsey, the heavyweight champion, was the toughest man in the world. Into their limelight stepped Grange.

Grange crossed an invisible line, from gentleman amateur/college athlete to professional football player. The public hungered to see more of Grange, and in 1925, when the Illini completed its season, he was happy to exploit his own name. Purists either attacked him for going commercial, or as in the case of his coach and father, expressed disappointment. But Papa Bear Halas understood something beyond the basic facts of the moment. He realized that Grange could be the vehicle to put pro football on the map with a much larger audience. Grange was ready made. He was an instant headliner.

It particularly vexed Halas that few fans comprehended the quality of professional play and failed to recognize that the older, bigger, more mature pros could bend, fold, and mutilate the lesser-experienced college teams into pretzels. It would take some time before that image was established and the hardliners who loved college football would permit the old, ingrained viewpoint to vanish.

In the meantime Halas could hitch his Bears wagon to the tail of a comet. Enter Charles "C. C." Pyle, also known as Cash and Carry Pyle, a promoter par excellence who had a vision of the possibilities and the energy to make a daring scheme pay off for everyone. Pyle, who owned a chain of movie theaters, had an intermediary approach for Grange while he was watching a film. In a brief meeting he proposed a barnstorming tour, guaranteeing Grange a sixty-forty split of profits that would make him at least $100,000. The deal ended up fifty-fifty for Pyle-Grange and the Bears and sixty-forty Grange from his partnership share with Pyle. Not to worry. There was plenty of cash to go around on this one.

In the course of his earlier life, Pyle had been a boxer, actor, salesman of neckties, and owner of nickelodeons. In the future he would organize the Bunion Derby, a 3,422-mile run from Los

Angeles to New York. However, at this magical moment in time, he turned himself into a sports agent, representing one Red Grange. His pitch was simple: Stick with me, boy, and you'll make a bunch of money. If some might be wary of hitching their good names to a huckster, Grange was willing to take the plunge.

Pyle offered a remarkable deal. Grange signed with Pyle only twenty-four hours after his final Illinois game, agreeing to go on a ten-game, seventeen-day tour across the country with the Chicago Bears. Halas was a salesman, too, and he realized what he had. Advertising began appearing: SEE RED GRANGE AND THE CHICAGO BEARS. Bears attendance zoomed from 5,000 or so a game to many times that.

When Grange suited up in his fresh blue-and-orange attire for the Bears on Thanksgiving Day 1925, against the Chicago Cardinals, some 36,000 fans chose football over turkey. These days, that is a common occurrence. At the time, it was unheard of.

Halas, quite the idea man himself, bowed to Pyle's superior gamesmanship, writing of the barnstorming plan, "It was a powerful idea. I would never have dared think of such a sweeping enterprise. But Pyle had unlimited vision."

Grange enjoyed the fame and celebrity that football provided, but above all he appreciated the security his pay offered. Always sincere, Grange never pretended that he was the circuit-riding Bear that autumn for fun or adventure. He candidly admitted that he did it for the money. Back in college, Grange said, he didn't have money to take girls on dates.

"I was a green country punk who stagged most of the time in college because I seldom had 15 cents to buy a girl a soda," he said.

This was like winning the lottery for Grange. His first check was for $25,000, and this is when the purists first expressed their displeasure over the college idol's selling out. Overnight Grange was transformed from a typical college guy scraping for cash to a big-time spender with money instead of holes in his pockets. Years later, he observed, "I went from having nothing to owning two or three cars at a time. I wore a raccoon coat. If something I ordered didn't cost $20, I didn't want it. I had a chance to make some money, a lot of money." And he grabbed it.

Pyle turned out to be as fabulous a promoter for Grange as P. T. Barnum was for the circus. He was no fly-by-night operator who took the box office proceeds and ran. He ran right alongside Grange to the bank, but Grange had the opportunity to make deposit after deposit himself. Nowadays, Americans are bombarded by full-page ads in magazines, one-minute ads on television, preview ads in movie theaters, resounding jingles on radio, and sales deals on cereal boxes. If a new children's movie hits the theaters, it generally features a tie-in with figurines at a fast-food chain. If a sports team wins a championship, only moments pass before caps and T-shirts can be ordered via 1-800 phone numbers.

But no one had seen the like in the 1920s. When Pyle took Grange pro and unleashed his ghostly presence on a wider American public, sports fans not only came out to see him run masterfully with the Chicago Bears, they were able to buy a variety of souvenirs. Available for their perusal were Red Grange dolls, cigars, ginger ale, and a line of clothing. Pyle and Grange reportedly split $500,000 as a result of the wild tour—at 1920s values. At the time there was no income tax, either. Grange discovered very quickly it was lucrative being Red Grange. He would gallop anywhere for the bucks, and it paid off handsomely.

Grange's first time in the lineup for the Bears was that Thanksgiving 1925 game against the Cardinals. It was not a debut to make fans forget his Michigan efforts. Grange rushed for under 40 yards, and the result was a 0–0 tie. But for once a football player did not have to wait a week to redeem himself. The exhibition route continued three days later. Grange rushed for 140 yards, and the Bears defeated the Columbus Tigers 14–13.

During one lull on the tour when the players weren't sleeping or eating, a famous incident occurred. An Illinois senator sent a limousine to pick up the wildly popular Grange and his new coach, Halas, and he delivered them to the White House for a brief audience with President Calvin Coolidge. When it came to football knowledge, Coolidge was no Richard Nixon, who once provided a play for the Washington Redskins that was called in a game. When Grange and Halas were introduced to the president as representing the Chicago Bears, Coolidge said, "Glad to meet you young gentlemen. I have always admired animal acts."

Later, the Bears played before 73,000 in the Polo Grounds in New York, and 75,000 watched the team play in Los Angeles. In New York, Babe Ruth stopped by to see the highly publicized Grange and offered some advice about fame.

"Don't pay too much attention to what they say about you, and don't pick up too many checks," the Bambino reportedly suggested.

Grange and pro football were on their way. Although the three-week period of Grange displaying his wares across the nation was transitory, a supernova of bright-lights attention, neither Grange nor pro football would ever be the same.

Halas told newspapermen that the all-star crowds that showed up to see the Bears and Grange on tour solidified his confidence that professional football would become "big time."

When the tour was over, however, Halas had no hold on Grange. Their deal expired. Given the riches earned, it was no wonder that Grange cast his lot with Pyle for a little bit longer. Pyle sought his own expansion franchise in New York, but the New York Giants and the Mara family owners were in no mood to share what still seemed like shaky professional territory.

So Pyle formed his own league, the American Football League, and Grange spent a season gallivanting from the backfield of the New York Yankees temporary football team. The league lasted just one season, the Yankees were absorbed into the National Football League, and the name was forevermore associated solely with baseball. Ironically, Grange suffered a serious knee injury playing against the Bears, an injury that permanently rendered his ghostlike running more like Casper than the Galloping Ghost.

Instead of inhabiting any football roster, Grange spent the 1928 season making movies and appearing on the vaudeville circuit. For some athletic stars, the vaudeville circuit was the equivalent of the current-day talk-show circuit, where all they had to do was show up and be themselves. In addition to appearing in a documentary, *The Galloping Ghost*, Grange found himself acting in two silent movies, *One Minute to Play* and *Racing Romeo*. But he did not consider acting to be his main talent.

Halas never forgot Grange's running skills and re-signed him to a real player contract for the 1929 season. Although his gimpy knee never again allowed Grange to approach the speed and cuts

Chicago Bears: Retired Numbers

3 — Bronko Nagurski
5 — George McAfee
7 — George Halas
28 — Willie Galimore
34 — Walter Payton
40 — Gale Sayers
41 — Brian Piccolo
42 — Sid Luckman
51 — Dick Butkus
56 — Bill Hewitt
61 — Bill George
66 — Clyde "Bulldog" Turner
77 — Harold "Red" Grange

he displayed at the height of his ability at Illinois, he spent until 1935 in the Bears lineup as both an offensive and defensive back and later a wide receiver.

His professional stats were quite respectable: 4,514 yards gained and 56 touchdowns scored.

Grange remained with the Bears as an assistant coach for a while, then owned a Chicago night club and sold insurance before returning to the sport that made him famous, working as a broadcaster on Bears games. It was a serendipitous reunion of one renowned ballplayer with the team he helped establish on firm footing.

True to his modest manner, when Grange gave a speech in 1978 where others were fawning over him, he said, "Hell, I'm not that great. I'm just an ordinary guy."

Yet the reason Red Grange endures in memory and why he remains a legend in the football world is that he was *far* from ordinary. What Grange did on the field made others gush. What Grange did for the Bears and professional football while becoming the sport's first true celebrity, helped define an era and bridge a perilous period for the game with its more prosperous future.

The Galloping Ghost may have been the finest pure runner of his time, the nearly invisible presence to tacklers who grabbed at air. But he became nationally famous because hundreds of thousands watched him so vividly do what opponents couldn't see.

Monsters of the Midway

The big man came from the north, and he was the biggest, baddest grizzly of them all. When normally solitary bears gather at a feeding spot, such as a salmon river, it is usually quickly understood which one of them is the boss. The one with the largest incisors, sharpest claws, and loudest growl marches through the territory unchallenged, its big shoulders rolling with each step. Others part or flee.

In 1930, such a bruiser appeared on the scene in the Chicago Bears lineup. Bronko

Bronko Nagurski was one of the toughest and greatest Bears, helping lift the team to early titles in the 1930s. *George Brace Collection*

Nagurski, the rugged fullback and linebacker, was so tough, so strong, so outsized in power that he intimidated all of those either futilely trying to tackle him when he tucked the ball under his arm or hopelessly seeking to block him when he charged the quarterback.

Nagurski was born on November 3, 1908, to Ukrainian immigrants who had moved to Ontario, Canada, just north of the Minnesota border. When he was four, they moved to International Falls, often referred to as the coldest place in the United States south of Alaska. Nagurski grew to 6'2" and 230 pounds at a time when most football linemen's weights hovered in the low 200s. In addition, Nagurski had a 22-inch neck and a size 19 ring finger. When a manufacturer measured Nagurski's finger for a championship ring, the officials said it was going to be the biggest ever made in the country. He was a behemoth, a Superman of chiseled muscle.

Nagurski teased those who shivered at the minus-fifty-degree weather of International Falls. He reveled in the image of himself as tough enough to withstand anything. Who knows, perhaps he was also just playing the psyche game with opponents.

"We don't have summer," he said. "We just have a season in the middle of the year when the sledding is poor."

Even now, those who endure winters in International Falls are admired for their grit. Years ago, Ernie Nevers, another great fullback of the era, responded to Nagurski's comments about a winter stretch of thirty straight days of ten-below temperatures. "No wonder you were so tough," Nevers said. "You had to be to survive."

Legends about Nagurski's power took many forms. Halas talked on camera years after Bronko's retirement about his out-running an entire defense, running right through the end zone and crashing into a brick wall. "That crack is still there," Halas said, laughing.

Nagurski played college football at the University of Minnesota, where his coach, Dr. Clarence Spears, felt the big guy was almost impossible to tackle. "When you hit him at the ankles," Spears said, "it is like getting an electric shock. If you hit him above the ankles, you're likely to get killed."

If the pros were used to digesting hyperbole from collegiate coaches and then proving them wrong, it was swiftly apparent that Nagurski's toughness transcended the amateur game. New York Giants coach Steve Owen uttered the famous description of Nagurski as "the only back I ever saw that ran his own interference." Nagurski was like a bowling ball knocking over pins.

Of course, this was the type of player George Halas salivated over. Nagurski fit his image of what a Bear should be on the gridiron, and he had to have him on his team. Nagurski joined the Bears in 1930, and it was no coincidence that his teaming with Red Grange helped Chicago dominate the early portion of the decade.

This is when the Chicago Bears were christened "The Monsters of the Midway." The center of the midway at the World's Columbian Exposition in 1893—or the Chicago World's Fair, as it came to be called in some quarters—was located on the south side of the city near the University of Chicago. The university, which played big-time college football until a school president deemphasized the sport, were the original claimants to the nick-

The First Draft

George Halas was selfish on behalf of his Chicago Bears—to a point. He wanted them to be the best, felt they always should be contending for the title, and wanted them to be the best recognized franchise in the National Football League.

But Halas also realized, even in the 1930s when like most Americans, he had trouble paying his bills, that it was not in the sport's best interest if one team dominated indefinitely. He wanted to grow the fan base for pro football, not kill it. So although at the time Halas wielded so much influence he probably could have organized defeat of a proposal to distribute young players equitably around the league, he chose to embrace a player draft.

The first draft of collegiate players took place in 1936, and the first first-round draft pick in the history of the Bears was a winner—tackle Joe Stydahar from West Virginia. Stydahar played for the Bears between 1936 and 1942 and again in 1945 and 1946 after his playing career was interrupted by World War II.

Linemen were growing. Stydahar, who was known as "Jumbo Joe," stood 6'4" and weighed 245 pounds. He was also an assistant coach under Halas with the 1963 Bears championship team before being inducted into the Pro Football Hall of Fame in 1967.

name. As time went on, the dominating Bears enthusiastically embraced the transfer of the phrase. It had historical ties, and it fit the picture of the rough-and-tumble, growling team that had its way with the rest of the National Football League.

The stock market crashed in 1929, the nation was plunged into the Great Depression, and the Bears slumped briefly for the first time, too, with a losing record. In stepping aside as coach for the first of four times in a six-decade-plus association with the team, Halas hired a former Illinois assistant coach, Ralph Jones. Playing Nagurski and Grange in the same backfield, Jones coaxed a 9–4–1 record out of the Bears in 1930. This was also the first season for future Hall of Fame end Bill Hewitt, who always played without the protection of the leather helmets in use.

In 1932, the Bears met the Portsmouth (Ohio) Spartans (the forerunners of the Detroit Lions) in their first NFL championship game and prevailed, 9–0. There was no planned title game that year, but the teams had tied during the regular season. In a bizarre twist, the game was the first football contest of consequence to be played indoors. The Bears had played one exhibition inside, and arena football was decades in the future, with its shorter dimension fields, but the championship encounter going indoors was more a reflection of necessity than innovation. Heavy snowfall and brutal winter conditions convinced the teams to play at Chicago Stadium, home of the hockey Blackhawks and future home of the basketball Bulls.

The horrible weather and frigid cold made Halas nervous. In the Bears' final regular-season game at Wrigley Field, only 5,000 fans turned out on another arctic-type day. Halas worried nobody would come to the championship game if conditions were worse.

Icy weather forced the NFL championship game indoors at Chicago Stadium in 1932, when the Bears defeated the Portsmouth Spartans (the future Detroit Lions) on a short field. Chicago Tribune Archives

Halas, the Spartans management, and league officials agreed to go indoors. The strategy at least helped attract nearly 12,000 fans to the game.

The field was only 80 yards long instead of 100 and only 40 yards wide instead of 53. Also, the circus had just been in town, and the coating of dirt and leftovers from the animals provided an unwelcome landing in several spots. It was not a game to be remembered for its artistry, but the Bears, boasting a defense that regularly recorded shutouts, needed just one score to win the title.

Fittingly, the fourth-quarter touchdown play involved Grange and Nagurski. Grange was kicked in the head in the game's first quarter and knocked unconscious. He was still woozy, but he went back into the lineup when it mattered. At the time, league rules required a passer to be located at least 5 yards behind the line of scrimmage, and this regulation played a part in the denouement.

The Portsmouth defense expected Nagurski to plunge with the pigskin, utilizing his power to bull to the goal line. Quarterback Carl Brumbaugh did hand off to Nagurski, but instead of running, Nagurski flipped the ball over the line to a wide-open Grange for a 2-yard touchdown. Immediately, the play was harshly challenged as a violation of the 5-yard rule. The Spartans were furious, but the TD stood. The Bears kicked the extra point and then scored on a safety for the final score. "I hadn't passed the ball at all at Minnesota or in high school," Nagurski said.

Months later, the play served as a catalyst for a rules change. From then on a passer could throw from anywhere behind the line of scrimmage. It helped to open up play and shape the NFL.

It would be nice to say that Halas was gracious in claiming his first championship in eleven years. However, before the game he taunted Spartans coach Potsy Clark because he was missing his best player, Dutch Clark, who had left the team for a higher-paying job. And during the game, when Coach Clark realized the Bears were stealing his signals, Halas taunted him about that.

Late in the game, with victory clinched, a gloating Halas actually stuck out his foot and tripped a Spartans player on the field running past the Bears bench.

Jones had promised to provide Halas with a championship within three seasons, and he delivered. He promptly resigned as coach and became athletic director at Lake Forest College. Halas was back on the sidelines for the 1933 season and directed the team to its second straight championship. This was the year Halas pioneered the use of film to study games. The Bears, who were 10–2–1, finished the season with five straight triumphs. Then they began the 1934 season with thirteen wins in a row. The mark of eighteen straight regular-season wins stood as a National Football League team record until the New England Patriots broke it in 2004.

The 1933 title game resembled the 1932 encounter in only the most basic of ways—both of them involved football. This time the Bears faced the New York Giants, a team that over the decades proved both foil and partner in remarkably memorable NFL games. Like the Bears, the Giants were one of the oldest franchises in the league. Like the Bears, the Giants regularly rose to the top of the standings. And like the Bears, the Giants were a family-run operation, a team handed down from generation to generation by the Mara clan. Wellington Mara, one of the great league patriarchs, and regarded as a titan of the sport, was involved with the team from the time he was fourteen until his death at age eighty-nine in 2005.

The Bears won their second consecutive title in Chicago in a marvelously played 23–21 game. This, too, was a game contested in bitter cold, but the teams stayed outdoors. The NFL had split its league into two divisions, and this was the first game pitting clubs from two divisions against one another to settle a championship. It was the Super Bowl of its time, long before there was an official Super Bowl. Naturally, the title game was created because the owners thought it would be a financial boon.

Some 26,000 fans were attracted to a game worth freezing for. The Bears led 9–7. The Giants led 14–9. The Bears led 16–14. The Giants led 21–16. The back-and-forth battle featured two touchdown tosses from Nagurski, and the Bears finally won on a highlight-film play that left fans stunned and giddy. "The greatest game I ever saw," Grange said.

In the fourth quarter, the Bears advanced to the Giants 33 yard line. Nagurski carried the ball and the line with him into New York territory. When he was given the ball again, he fooled the defense by stopping and throwing a jump pass to end Hewitt. Hewitt, easily distinguishable in the crowd downfield because his hair flowed freely without a helmet, plucked the ball out of the air. He turned to the Giants goal line but was about to be tackled. So he lateraled to trailing Bill Karr on the right sideline. Karr was surrounded and about to go down when Bear Gene Ronzani unleashed a phenomenal block to deck both defenders. Karr scored, covering the last 19 yards, and the Bears led with a minute to go. The Giants tried a last-ditch pass play that was completed. But Grange anticipated a lateral and broke up the play to end the game by tackling the ball carrier high, so he couldn't make the flip.

Grange was great but past his prime. It was Nagurski that opponents feared the most at the time. The rival Giants knew that he was the one who had to be shut down for them to over-

Bronko Nagurski has a big hole to run through here, but he often made his own holes. George Brace Collection

take the Bears. "I was never hit so hard in my life as one time when I tried to stop him in the open field," said 1930s Giants quarterback Harry Newman. "I hit him as hard as I could, and all it did was knock him off pace a little."

Giants coach Steve Owen suggested Nagurski was too powerful to be stopped by normal means. "Defense him?" said Owen. "There's one defense that could stop him. Shoot him before he leaves the dressing room."

Nobody, however, summarized the Bears' two champi-onships of the early 1930s more accurately or succinctly than the future Hall of Fame center George Trafton when the team was celebrating the second win at a bar. Trafton raised a glass and said, "Once again, a toast to the Ghost. But Nagurski, you're still the man with the most."

Many allusions were made to Nagurski as the Paul Bunyan of pro football. Grange always raved about his backfield partner's strength. And Minnesota's Coach Spears added to the lore. He told folks he recruited Nagurski after a visit to the north country, where he got lost. Supposedly, he saw the big fella plowing the field on the family farm and signed him up when Nagurski raised the plow and pointed as he gave Spears directions.

There was every reason to believe that the Bears were on the cusp of a dynasty. They had two championships in their pocket, and 1934's team was so awesome—recalling that the team won its first thirteen games in a row—that a third title seemed a formal-ity. Not only did Halas still have Nagurski and Grange, he dis-covered a new weapon that season.

Running back Beattie Feathers became the first player to rush for 1,000 yards in a season when he broke that barrier as a rookie. Feathers—who was quick, with a long stride, and made masterful cuts—collected 1,004 yards but was injured and out for the year by playoff time. Feathers averaged an astounding 8.4 yards per carry. What made Feathers's life so easy was that he had Nagurski blocking for him. It was like having a snowplow clear the street for your sedan.

That season the Bears scored 286 points to their opponents' 86. The defense recorded three shutouts and held eight other

"Scrooge" Halas

It has often been said that George Halas was a penny-pincher when it came to player salaries and that the resentment some of his 1950s and 1960s players felt would have been alleviated if he had been a bit more generous.

What helped determine Halas's outlook, however, was the fact that in their earliest days the Bears never were really flush. The National Football League as a whole was not a moneymaking operation in the 1920s, and just when it seemed the sport might turn the corner, the teams, like the rest of American society, were bludgeoned by the Great Depression.

In 1932, when Halas worried about the future of his beloved team, his partner, Dutch Sternaman, said he wanted out of pro football. With great difficulty, Halas raised $18,000 to buy out Sternaman.

Halas lived long enough to appreciate a substantial increase in the value of his team—to a level almost beyond belief. Once the era of network-television-rights support began, the team became worth millions and millions.

opponents to 10 points or less. When Chicago engaged the New York Giants in a return match for the title on December 9 at the Polo Grounds, there was no reason for Halas to think his team would fail to three-peat.

When the players awoke that day, it was also unlikely that they anticipated they would engage in one of the most famous games in National Football League history, either: the Sneaker Game. The day was wintry, but it became colder as time passed. Certain areas of the field were more forgiving than others. Some of the turf was passable; other places froze.

The Bears had taken a 13–3 lead at halftime, and given the way the season had unfolded, that seemed a comfortable enough margin. However, for once, an opposing coach outsmarted Halas. At halftime, the Giants' trainer, who also had ties to Manhattan College, made a dash across town, prevailed upon a guard to let him into the team's basketball locker room, and scooped up as many gym shoes as he could find. Nine Giants players emerged for the second half wearing rubber-soled shoes that offered far better traction on the icy field than any of the cleats the Bears wore on their feet.

Suddenly, the Bears were being outplayed. Bears defenders who made sure tackles in the first half slipped and slid doing pratfalls as Giants runners brushed past them. Giants players wearing the sneakers had the advantage. Infuriated as New York ran up 27 points in the fourth quarter, Halas shouted to his men, "Step on their toes!"

Such a retaliatory measure was an insufficient strategy. The Bears fell to the Giants, 30–13. It was a maddening way to lose, failing in the battle of wits rather than in the battle of football skill. This was the last roundup for Grange. He retired after the 1934 season. "Every football player knows when his time is up," Grange said. Nagurski made the choice to retire after the 1937 season (though he would be heard from again), and although the

Bears had successful seasons for the rest of the decade, they were in transition.

Halas searched for a new offensive weapon that could match the explosiveness of the Grange-Nagurski tandem. A man could wait a lifetime for such a miracle find. But if Halas was impatient by nature, he was also the lord of his manor. He knew that someday a prince would come along who could help him rule the league again.

Bitter Rivals

For sale, $2.00 bumper stickers: PACKERSSUCK.COM. WHY? 'CUZ THEY DO!

Papa Bear Halas would probably laugh. This is the modern-day outlet for Chicago Bears fans and others who hate the Green Bay Packers. Booing, the old-fashioned way of expressing displeasure when Curly Lambeau brought the Wisconsin rivals to Wrigley Field, is insufficient when the teams are not actually engaged in gridiron combat.

Now there is a Web site—sign on any time, and interact with kindred spirits who also despise the Packers—24/7, around the calendar, not just in autumn when the National Football Conference North Division plays home and home each year.

Come one, come all, tell us how you really feel: Packers Suck One-Liner number 1: "What's the difference between a Green Bay Packer fan and a carton of yogurt? The yogurt has culture."

Packers Suck One-Liner number 2: "Why do people from Green Bay go to Lambeau when there is a tornado warning? Because there are no touchdowns there."

Packers Suck One-Liner number 3: "What do you call a row of Packer fans lined up ear to ear? A wind tunnel!"

It should be noted that the superior attitude goes both ways. Packers fans have their own anti-Bears Web sites to read for feel-good messages of hatred. And outside Lambeau Field before games, season-ticket-holder Jeff Karll operates a booth that specializes in selling $17 T-shirts reading BEARS STILL SUCK. The Bears don't even have to be the opponent that day.

In a 2005 *Chicago Tribune* story pointing out that the feelings still run strong regardless of where the teams are situated in the standings, a song recorded more than fifteen years before by the Happy Schnapps Combo was cited as repeating twenty-six times, "Bears Still Suck." It is easy to tell that it was penned during a period when the Bears had the upper hand, because the song suggests it would be a good thing if Mike Ditka was run over by a truck. One juicy stanza referring to a field trip from Wisconsin to Chicago goes, "If you drive to Soldier Field, they make you pay a toll; for cripes' sake they only won one Super Bowl." Touché.

Bears and Packers fans have had a long time to get on one another's nerves. The first meeting in the Bears–Packers series took place in 1921, when the Bears were still the Staleys. Decatur won 20–0. In the eighty-four years from then to the 2005 season,

Bears–Packers Stats that Don't Figure

Fans of the Chicago Bears and fans of the Green Bay Packers like to think of themselves as the hardiest in the National Football League. The wind blows off Lake Michigan into Soldier Field and can make November, December, and January games in downtown Chicago quite uncomfortable. Green Bay is so far north in Wisconsin that the temperatures might drop twenty-five degrees lower on any given Sunday than they are in Chicago.

So it is ironic that since 1970, when the Bears gave up Wrigley Field and moved into Soldier Field, three of the four smallest crowds to watch the team play were recorded against the Packers.

The smallest of all gatherings to witness a Bears football game during that period showed up only 19,157 strong on December 16, 1973. The third fewest number of spectators was the 33,557 for the December 11, 1977, Packer game in Chicago. And the fourth smallest crowd was the 34,306 that turned out for the December 10, 1978, Packers game at Soldier Field.

The one thing all of the games had in common? They were all played on cold days in December.

One other irony in the rivalry. The two teams have met only once in a playoff situation. On December 14, 1941, a week after the bombing of Pearl Harbor, the Bears defeated the Packers 33–14 at Wrigley Field to win the conference championship.

There had been a tie for the Western Conference championship, and the Bears prevailed. Then the Bears met the New York Giants for the league title. At no other time in the next sixty-five years would the Bears and Packers be a postseason obstacle for the other team's march to a title.

the teams played 169 times, and the Bears led the series 85–78, with six ties.

Chicago is only 45 miles from the Wisconsin border, and Green Bay is only a two-and-a-half-hour drive from Chicago. The teams are practically neighbors. Residents on both sides of the state line *are* neighbors. There really is no demilitarized zone; if you live north of the Illinois border, you are for the Packers, and if you live south of the Wisconsin border, you are for the Bears— unless your families were silly enough to move to the other denomination.

Although George Halas had great respect for Curly Lambeau (who eventually had the Packers stadium named for him) and later Vince Lombardi, it was always something special to the Bears patriarch to beat the Packers. Maybe it was the familiarity. But there is little doubt that for decades this has been the longest and hottest NFL rivalry.

Johnny "Blood" McNally, a Pro Football Hall of Fame running back for the Packers in the 1930s, recalled how the team psyched itself up for meetings with the Bears by chanting, "Bear meat is mighty sweet. Bears are hard to beat. Let's lead them to defeat."

Great sports figures need great rivals to bring out their best. Champions are most admired when they defeat other greats. Muhammad Ali's ultimate fighting reputation was forged by his outlasting Joe Frazier twice. Chris Evert and Martina Navratilova battled head to head in tennis tournament finals for years. Bill Russell had Wilt Chamberlain as an equal giant. The New York Yankees and Boston Red Sox engage in some of the fiercest baseball games year after year.

Bears running back Anthony "A Train" Thomas (35) bulls for yardage while dragging a Green Bay defender in a 2001 game. Chicago Tribune Archives

In many instances it is possible to be a fan of the games, a purist sports fan who derives pleasure from the matchups. But it is almost impossible to be a fan of both sides. You are a Red Sox fan or a Yankees fan. You are an Ali champion or a Frazier sympathizer. There are no Bears and Packers fans inhabiting the same body.

When Lovie Smith took over as the Bears head coach in 2004, the first goal he described was beating the Packers. It warmed the hearts of Bears fans who may have thought the team, its players, and coaches had perhaps gone a little soft in recent years, calling the twice-a-year Packers matches just another game.

The Bears were a target for the Packers because the Bears won more games, won more championships, and garnered more national attention—until Lombardi took over and won five titles in seven years in the mid-1960s. Boy, did it frost Bears fans when Green Bay residents referred to themselves as inhabitants of "Titletown." Heck, it was enough that the Packers, situated in a community of 60,000 or so fans, the NFL's smallest, could tweak the Bears over anything.

Fred "Fuzzy" Thurston, a star lineman on Lombardi's great teams and the owner of a bar in Green Bay, said the Packers became the true America's team, not the Dallas Cowboys. Everyone who lived in a small town could identify with the Pack, he said.

During various periods of time, each team exerted dominance. The Lombardi era tipped the edge to the Packers. When Mike Ditka became the Bears coach in 1982, he understood where Bears fans' hearts lay. Crush the Packers. Devour the Packers. Conveniently for Ditka, who played in the early sixties, the Packers were coached by their great guard Forrest Gregg, who also played in the sixties. Ditka suffered enough as a player during the Lombardi period; he made it clear to his guys that they were not going to repeat history. A preseason game in 1984 set the tone for the Ditka-Gregg coaching period. Gregg got so angry at Ditka he wanted to choke him. The teams discontinued playing exhibition games.

"Mike Ditka and Forrest Gregg played against each other, and they hated each other," said Keith Van Horne, who played tackle on the Bears 1986 Super Bowl team under Ditka's tutelage. "So that carried over to the players. You can imagine that the rivalry was certainly emphasized.

"He [Ditka] cranked it up a notch with Green Bay. He just could not stand them and could not stand Forrest Gregg, let me tell you. Gregg was a great player, but as a coach, to entice your players to wear towels with people's numbers on them for hits is just cheap. I think as a coach he was an embarrassment to the Green Bay Packers organization. If I ever met him, I'd let him know that, too."

And Van Horne was speaking a dozen years into retirement, so it is not as if the Bears' feelings about the rivals mellow with age.

In 1985 Ditka first employed William "Refrigerator" Perry as a colossal running back against the Packers. Perhaps to show them up? The then-ferocious Bears defense, on its way to Super Bowl triumph, also KO'd two Packer quarterbacks in the same game.

Don Pierson, the *Chicago Tribune's* longtime professional football writer, reported an astonishing incident when the Bears visited Lambeau later that same season. Accompanied by a note from a Wisconsin radio station reading, "Here's what you guys are full of," the Bears locker room contained a bag of excrement stinking up the closed-in changing area.

Tim Wrightman, a tight end who played two seasons for the Bears in the mid-1980s, including the Super Bowl championship year, said the Packers "were probably the dirtiest team that we played. It's the only time I've ever been in games where I got hit in the nuts. They were just trying to overcome their lack of talent.

"It was always very hard, just really hard, even though we won all four games I played. But when you played them, you always had to have your head on a swivel."

If you didn't, Wrightman said, you might get clobbered from behind and injured.

The Ditka-Gregg era was characterized by games where six personal-foul penalties were whistled in a first half and when quarterback Jim McMahon waved his middle finger at Gregg. Now those were the good old days. Sounds more like *Slapshot* hockey than pro football.

It has always been considered important for a Bears coach's longevity to win against the Packers. On December 25, 1998, when Dave Wannstedt was on the ropes as coach of the Bears, this headline appeared in the *Chicago Tribune:* BEATING THE PACK COULD SAVE WANNSTEDT'S JOB. Merry Christmas.

At the time Wannstedt had lost nine straight times to the Packers. That is the type of streak that will get you fired. The team had to be groping for any kind of holiday present if it was suggested a single victory over the Packers could salvage a career. Things got so bad that Packer fans were able to buy tickets to games in Chicago at Soldier Field and had the gall to show up wearing team colors. One Bears team official termed the outfits (no doubt topped off with cheesehead hats) "the sickening green and gold."

Paul Hornung, the great Packers running back of the early 1960s, who still owns the NFL's single-season scoring record of 176 points, totaled in just twelve games, said the Packers reveled in their success over the Bears from the big city. "We got a lot more publicity in the Midwest when we beat the Bears," Hornung said.

The Bears' big problem from the early 1990s on was Packer quarterback Brett Favre. The future Hall of Fame quarterback always seemed to pull tricks out of his helmet to prevail. He beat the Bears with an injured leg and an injured thumb. In twenty-five games against Chicago going into the 2005 campaign, Favre's record was 20–5.

A couple of years ago, then Bears defensive tackle Bryan Robinson did not equivocate when asked about Favre's impact on the series. "Brett Favre is the man, no question," he said.

Gary Fencik, a retired Bears defensive back who still lives in the Chicago area, said Favre is responsible for diminishing the rivalry in an unexpected way—he's too good.

"I think in order to have a good rivalry you have to have a little more balance," said Fencik, another Super Bowl veteran. "Unfortunately, the Bears haven't really been a good foil for the Packers since Brett Favre became their quarterback."

Ahh, the Favre Syndrome. The firm view that Favre has the Bears' number isn't going to cause any Chicago news show to break into regularly scheduled programming. However, in 2005 the Packers' record was only 2–9 by the time they first faced the Bears. Favre said, "I'm sure people in Chicago are tickled to death with the Packers."

Green Bay quarterback Brett Favre is the man who haunted more than a decade's worth of Bears defenders' dreams. *Chicago Tribune Archives*

No Sympathy for Favre

The symbol of the new world order—at least from a Bears fan's point of view—was the December 4, 2005, domination of the Packers. For once, quarterback Brett Favre had no miracle comebacks lurking in his right arm.

The final score was 19–7, but the victory felt far more emphatic. Instead of leading his team over the Bears with late touchdown passes, Favre suffered three interceptions. Instead of marching his team down the field, Favre was chased all over the neighborhood by Bears defenders.

Favre looked every inch his thirty-six years and probably felt a decade older. When he met the press an hour after the Bears' destruction, he limped on his right side, and his right hand and arm were packaged in thick bandages. He also said he was kicked in the right shin. "Tonight and tomorrow, it will be really sore," Favre said. "It's nothing I can't handle. You find out how tough you are."

If Favre had any thought that Bears fans might feel his pain, he would have been sadly mistaken. When Chicago sports-talk-show hosts asked callers if they had any sympathy for Favre, the fans who had seen him whip their team so often were blunt. "No!" they responded.

They were more gleeful after the Bears swept the Packers. The Bears took out the Packers 19–7 in Chicago, with the defense hounding Favre all game long. Then the Bears took sweeter revenge on Green Bay and Favre by beating their tormentors 24–17 in Wisconsin on Christmas Day.

In recent years, with free agency, players have changed teams with much more frequency than they did in past decades. Some of the most famous Bears of the mid-1980s rather amazingly found themselves playing out the end of their careers in Green Bay. McMahon and defensive tackle Steve McMichael were two passionate Bears who were unlikely candidates to ever wear Packer green and gold, but they did.

What remains inconceivable is that Mike Ditka would ever cash a paycheck from the Green Bay Packers organization. He probably wouldn't even be seen driving through the community; if he did, Ditka might find himself the object of scorn on Packerssuck.com.

Packers Suck One-Liner number 4: "Why are the Packers all buying microscopes? It's the only way they can still see their Super Bowl chances."

Packers Suck One-Liner number 5: "How do a newborn puppy and a Packers fan differ? A newborn puppy stops whining after a week."

Packers Suck One-Liner number 6: "Why does Lambeau Field have natural grass? The cheerleaders need somewhere to graze."

It must be a great comfort to Forrest Gregg and all Packer fans to read the accompanying Packerssuck.com disclaimer:

> Packers Suck Dot Com is a website that is not to be taken seriously. The opinions and views of the editorial staff are only opinions and views and are of a joking matter. With what has transpired in 2001, humor is needed to tame the horror that is happening in our

world. If anyone has any reason to believe that these pages are off-color, in poor-taste, or if any of these pages infuriate you or hurt your feelings. . . Please RELAX. This is only a joke.

No employee of a detective agency will be surprised to discover that Packerssuck.com originates in Illinois.

Sid the Savior

The worst slaughter in National Football League history provided a primer on avoiding bulletin-board material at all costs. If anyone wonders why football coaches worry about pregame trash talking, lesson number one offers the answer from the most lopsided pro game of them all. Washington Redskins owner George Preston Marshall should have kept his mouth shut prior to his team's 1940 championship game against the Chicago Bears.

Washington defeated the Bears 7–3 during the regular season. That was all the evidence Marshall needed to support his belief that hosting the title game would overcome anything the Bears mustered. Marshall had Slingin' Sammy Baugh as his quarterback, one of the greatest all-around players in league history. To Marshall, the Bears represented the past, a golden bygone era. It was time for his team to be recognized as the next dynasty.

Following the Redkins victory, Marshall said, "The Bears are a team that folds under pressure in the second half against a good team. If they come down here to play us in the championship game, they'll have to win by a big score or they won't win at all."

Marshall's overconfidence was a mouthful. His demeanor was arrogant. It was his team's time, and he was sure of it. George Halas saw the newspaper story quoting Marshall, cut it out, and pasted it on his team's locker room wall without saying a word. Each day as they practiced leading up to the title game, the Bears walked past the offending comments and growled. They understood that Halas put the story there to be read, to be digested, and to be answered the best way they knew how.

On game day at Griffith Stadium—a clear afternoon on December 8, 1940—Halas uttered his final pep talk. Then he whipped out a copy of the story and for the first time vented. "Gentlemen," he said, "this is what George Preston Marshall and the Redskins think of you."

The Bears had finished the regular season 8–3 in 1940, a fine record but not nearly one of their best. Yet that day Halas told his men he thought they were the greatest group of football players of all time. Clearly, they fell for it—and they likely played the greatest game of all time.

Chicago scored first. Bill Osmanski ran 68 yards for a touchdown on the Bears' second play from scrimmage. Shortly thereafter, for one of the few times all day, the Redskins had a golden scoring chance. A long pass from Baugh to Charley Malone at the goal line was dropped when the sun got in the receiver's eyes. After that, the Bears put up points almost as quickly as a pinball machine could tally them. At halftime, the Bears led 28–0. After three quarters, the Bears led 54–0. Since this was no softball game, the mercy rule was not in effect. The teams played on. The final score was 73–0.

The Bears' Gene Ronzani dashes through a big hole during the 1940 NFL championship game, a 73-0 rout of the Washington Redskins. *George Brace Collection*

There never has been another NFL game that approached such a humiliating score. Amusingly, the Bears scored so often that as time ran out officials were running short of footballs. It is said that when the gun sounded, ending the massacre, there was only one football available for use.

Famously, when reporters asked Baugh if Malone's bobble would have made a difference, he replied, "If Charley had caught the ball, the final score would have been 73–7."

Baugh made no excuses and was as clear as possible in emphasizing just how tremendous the Bears were that day. It was a case of everything working to perfection. And although the Bears' regular-season mark was short of some others, the team, as Halas observed, was probably as mighty as any assembled. Seven Bears who played on the 1940 title team were elected to the Hall of Fame: guard Danny Fortmann, lineman George Musso, tackle Joe Stydahar, end George McAfee, lineman Bulldog Turner, and quarterback Sid Luckman, plus Halas.

Fifty-seven years later, the *Chicago Tribune* arranged a panel to select the top 150 most memorable moments in Chicago sports history. The 73–0 wipeout ranked first.

Luckman was Halas's boy. Sid was like a son to Halas. From the first time Halas saw Luckman pass for Columbia University, he knew the young man could be the quarterback he needed to run an offense that in his mind was growing in sophistication. Halas traded with the Pittsburgh Steelers to obtain the NFL's number one draft pick in 1939.

And then he wrote to Luckman and discovered that he did not want to play pro football. Halas had Columbia coach Lou Little talk to Luckman on his behalf. Same answer. Halas wrote

Quarterback on a Pedestal

He may not be the most famous Bear to present-day fans, since he retired more than fifty-five years ago, but the late Sid Luckman might be the most important player in the history of the franchise. Not only did Luckman win four titles as quarterback of the Bears in the 1940s, but stunningly, in the entire history of the team, Luckman is the only great quarterback with any longevity.

In his twelve seasons as signal caller for the Bears, Luckman threw 137 touchdown passes, including a record 7 in one game, for just under 15,000 yards. His single-season quarterback rating of 107.8 in 1943 is a club record.

But Luckman is alone on a pedestal. Years ago, when a *Chicago Tribune* writer compiled a list of Bears bests and worsts, he called Luckman the team's greatest quarterback. His flip side, the Bears' worst quarterback, was "shared by many."

It is unfathomable that the Bears have had so few quarterbacks of note who turned in fabulous seasons. The colorful, brash Jim McMahon was at the helm for the Bears' 1986 Super Bowl championship. McMahon was the main man for seven seasons, but he also missed half of about four of them with injuries.

Jim Harbough was the starter for four seasons in the early 1990s and put up some good numbers. Erik Kramer had just two seasons where he made it through the entire schedule as the boss under center, but his 1995 campaign was a record setter. That year he set the team mark for attempts (522), completions (315), yards (3,838), and touchdown passes (29).

The Bears also received good leadership from Bill Wade between 1961 and 1966, Rudy Bukich in the late 1950s and again in the 1960s, and a little bit from Jim Miller between 1998 and 2002. But rarely have they had much consistency. From the second half of the 1990s to the present, because of incompetence or injury, the Bears have regularly started three different quarterbacks in a season. That pattern is not a recipe for winning in the NFL.

to Luckman again. Finally, Halas traveled to New York with a contract in his pocket, and after dining with Luckman and his new bride Estelle at their apartment, coaxed him into signing for $5,000-plus.

To Halas, paying that amount of money to a veteran hurt. Paying that type of cash to an untried rookie practically left him hyperventilating. But Halas knew that Luckman was the keymaster for his T-formation, and he had faith in his own judgment of talent. Halas needed Luckman, and the quarterback proved his value many times over.

Playing between 1939 and 1950, then acting as an assistant coach for many years, Luckman became the greatest quarterback in Bears history. Indeed, his prowess behind center for so long is not only unmatched in team history, it is unapproached. Halas was correct. Luckman was the perfect fit. He was a tremendous leader on the field. He could throw with anyone of the era, except perhaps Baugh. He had sound judgment. And his and Papa Bear's personalities clicked.

With Luckman at the helm, the Bears had their greatest decade. Not only did they put the world-class whupping on the Redskins in 1940, the Bears won world championships in 1941, crushing the Giants, 37–9 at Wrigley Field; in 1943, toppling the Redskins, 41–21, also in Chicago; and in 1946, polishing off the Giants again, 24–14, at the Polo Grounds.

Part of that time, Halas was a commander in the navy, off to distant ports. In 1943, the manpower shortage due to World War II provoked Halas into talking Bronko Nagurski into a comeback. Luckman expressed deep admiration for the older player and said

Sid Luckman is the greatest quarterback in Bears history and still holds many records, including 7 touchdown passes in one game.
George Brace Collection

Nagurski was so strong he couldn't imagine what the Bronk was like in his prime.

The title triumph over the Giants in 1941 was a true thrashing to cap a 10–1 regular season. It came only two weeks after Pearl Harbor, when the future of pro football, and the world, was uncertain. The Bears broke open a close game in the second half with 4 touchdowns.

The Bears, who went 11–0 in the regular season, also advanced to the 1942 title game but lost 14–6 to Washington, as the Redskins got their revenge for the embarrassment of 1940. Sammy Baugh was the hero, throwing a touchdown pass and also intercepting a pass in the end zone while playing defense. The Redskins did not need trumped-up bulletin-board material or insults from an owner for motivation. Washington Coach Ray Flaherty simply chalked the numbers "73–0" on his locker-room blackboard and walked away.

Nearly 400 players from recent rosters were in the American armed forces by the fall of 1943, and NFL owners debated about suspending the season. They voted to play, but many players were fill-ins. Nagurski came out of retirement, despite a body that was rusting at the joints. One thing that had not helped Nagurski in his years away from football was the professional wrestling he did. His body took a beating bouncing on the canvas and exchanging forearms and gouges with other human battering rams. He told his coach, Hunk Anderson, filling in for Halas, that he was so slow Anderson would "need a sundial to time me in the hundred."

Yet in Nagurski's one return season before retiring again to Minnesota, the Bears won the big prize. Luckman's arm was showcased in the 1943 victory over Washington. He threw 5 touchdown passes, 2 each to Harry Clark and Dante Magnani, and intercepted 3 passes. "Those are the things you dream about," Luckman said.

That season Luckman won the league's Most Valuable Player award, and in a regular-season game against the Giants, he threw 7 touchdown passes. More than sixty years later, the record has been tied but never broken.

In 1946, with the war over and veteran players who were also veteran soldiers filling rosters again, the Bears adapted well enough to capture their fourth championship of the decade. The Bears and Giants were tied 14–14 in the fourth quarter. New York believed Luckman was going to pass. But Luckman eluded the rush and fooled the defense with a 19-yard bootleg touchdown run to break open the game.

The Bears, the Giants, and the Redskins ruled the NFL during the war years, and Halas assumed his team was well positioned to win more titles when he returned to the sidelines. But 1946 was the last time Luckman led the Bears to a championship. When he retired in 1950, and in the ensuing years, Halas seemed well stocked with quarterbacks. Yet despite the remarkably good fortune to list George Blanda, Zeke Bratkowski, and Ed Brown on the roster at the same time, the Bears could never quite make things work. The Bears also let Bobby Layne go to the Detroit Lions, a major mistake.

There were some lean years. In 1952 the Bears finished 5–7, and in 1953 the Bears were 3–8–1. If there were whispers that the game had passed Papa Bear Halas by, they were just that. It did not pay to underestimate one of the founders of the league, certainly not out loud. By the mid-1950s the Bears were back as contenders and were being stocked with fresh faces who were top-notch players.

A Team in the Hall of Fame

Quarterback Sid Luckman was the Bears player of the decade in the 1940s, but his career overlapped with several Hall of Famers besides Bronko Nagurski.

Danny Fortmann, guard, 1936–43
As a rookie, Fortmann was the NFL's youngest starter at age 20. While playing for the Bears, Fortmann worked on his medical studies at the University of Chicago.

George Musso, tackle, guard, defensive tackle, 1933–44
Musso, team captain for eight seasons, was originally signed by George Halas for $90 a game, plus $5 in expenses.

George McAfee, running back, defensive end, 1940–41 and 1945–50
McAfee was a first-round draft pick of the Philadelphia Eagles, but Halas traded four players for him. McAfee excelled at punt returns and also intercepted 25 passes.

Joe Stydahar, tackle, 1936–42 and 1945–46
Big Joe was All-NFL four straight seasons and returned from World War II service in the navy to complete his career on the 1946 championship team.

Clyde "Bulldog" Turner, center, linebacker, 1940–52
Turner returned an interception 96 yards for a touchdown and in the 1942 season picked off 8 passes.

George Connor, tackle, linebacker, 1948–55
A three-time All-American at Holy Cross and Notre Dame, Connor was All-NFL five times before injuries ended his career.

Two-way lineman Stan Jones, a future Hall of Famer, came to the Bears out of the University of Maryland in 1954; fullback Rick Casares became a Bear in 1955 out of the University of Florida; and Doug Atkins, considered one of the strongest men ever to play for Chicago, joined the team in 1955 out of the University of Tennessee.

"I think I blocked him three times in nine years," Packers star halfback Paul Hornung said of Atkins. Yet Hornung called Casares "the toughest player in the NFL." The Bears were beginning to roar again.

One of the unlikeliest of Bears was end Harlon Hill, a small-college sensation from Florence State Teachers College in Alabama, drafted in 1954. Hill said neither he nor any of his teammates or small-college foes in the Deep South thought much about playing in the National Football League. There were no teams in the region, and televised football was almost nonexistent. "Nobody dreamed of it," he said.

Hill was playing in the old Blue-Gray All-Star game on Christmas Day in Montgomery, Alabama, and one coach told another coach who told Halas that Hill was the best end in the South. Halas telephoned Hill.

"I didn't think about pro football until Coach Halas called me," Hill said. "I didn't know much about pro football when I went up." Hill caught on fast. He became one of the Bears' top receivers, and with exceptional speed and the stride of a racehorse, he turned catches into big gains. In an era when passing had yet to take on the importance it has in recent years, Hill had an eye-opening rookie season. He caught 45 passes for 1,124 yards and 12 touchdowns. His average gain per catch was an astounding 25.0 yards. And although Hill's 233 total receptions over a ten-year career do not sound terribly impressive today, his 20.2 yards per catch average is notable.

By 1956, the Bears had reloaded. Rookie J. C. Caroline, a two-way back out of Illinois, was trying to fit in and saw early on that the Bears had the makings of a special team. "You started feeling the veterans were taking charge and kind of taking those rookies under the wing and giving direction and guidance," Caroline said. "A lot of the guys had just come out of college and were playing in a different bracket. Now you're playing with guys just as good as you are, or better."

The 1956 Bears, coached by Paddy Driscoll, compiled a 9–2–1 record. During the regular season the Bears and New York Giants tied 17–17. The two teams often seemed to be on the same cycle near the top of the league, and the two met once again for the championship. "The Giants, that was always a big game," Jones said. "Because they always had a lot of publicity in New York, and they had all those superstars on their team."

In a circumstance almost beyond belief, a demoralizing chapter in Bears history repeated itself. The Giants won the title 47–7, on December 30, 1956. Bad enough, but the way they took control was frustrating beyond all measure. This was Sneaker Game II. Same thing. An icy field, the Giants obtained sneakers, replaced their cleats, and ran all over the Bears. At least the Bears had some rubber-soled shoes of their own this time, even if they seemed to be Brand X. The Giants scored on fullback Mel Triplett's 17-yard run on their first possession and led 20–0 before the Bears made it onto the scoreboard.

New York Giants kicker Ben Agajanian boots a field goal in the 1956 championship game rout of the Bears at Yankee Stadium. *Chicago Tribune Archives*

"We kicked off to the Giants to open the game," said Casares, who scored the Bears' only touchdown on a 9-yard run. "They brought it back 52 yards, and our guys were sliding all over the place. They had traction, and our guys were sliding. We changed our cleats, but they just managed to grip."

Whether the Giants possessed superior tennis shoes or superior talent, the result was never in question. It would be seven long years before the Bears made it back to the title game, but by then almost all of those youngsters added to the roster in the mid-1950s had matured into star players and filled critical roles.

Champions Again

The men who did the tackling remember 1963 with pride and a belief that their reincarnation of the Monsters of the Midway is what brought a championship back to Chicago for the first time in seventeen years.

Fans may have been spoiled the way the Bears roughed up the National Football League for four titles in the 1940s. But neither they nor George Halas would imagine that no championship would be brought to the Windy City between 1946 and 1963. The Bears were titleless from the end of World War II to the start of the Beatles era. They were dry throughout the 1950s expansion of suburbia and the revolution of the early days of television. No championships came to Chicago following the integration of returning soldiers into NFL lineups through the Korean War and into the first stirrings of the Vietnam War.

During the robust 11–1–2 campaign of 1963, the Bears unleashed an old-time defense reminiscent of the previous trademark of the team. Monsters? Yes. Four decades ahead of time, the answer to the question, "Who let the dogs out?" was Old Man Halas. Over the course of a fourteen-game schedule, the Bears allowed only 144 points. They were stingier than Scrooge.

"We had a great defense," said Rich Pettibon, one of the warriors of the defensive backfield, who is retired in Virginia, following a long playing and coaching career. "Our offense was adequate. They didn't lose games, but they rarely won games. They just kept us in games, and our defense really dominated that year."

Seven times that season the Monsters held opposing teams to a single touchdown or less. The core of defenders included a phenomenal linebacking crew. The late Bill George anchored the middle and was flanked by Joe Fortunato and Larry Morris. "It sure was a great trio," said Fortunato, who lives in Natchez, Mississippi.

Although the entire unit was special, no one terrorized foes like defensive end Doug Atkins. Atkins, who stood 6'8" and weighed about 280 pounds in his prime, was in many quarters

Defensive end Doug Atkins was considered the strongest man in the NFL during his seventeen-season career. George Brace Collection

regarded as the strongest man in the league. Atkins was agile, with great leaping ability, and his combination of assets allowed him to practically live in enemy backfields. More than forty years later, Pettibon still marvels at the way Atkins disrupted opposing teams.

"It was a fourteen-game schedule, and I think Atkins knocked nine guys out," Pettibon said. "When I say knocked them out, I mean they were out. They carried them off, and they never came back."

This was the early 1960s, when the Green Bay Packers ruled the football world and to assemble a team their equal took considerable effort and skill from Halas. It took even more savvy because the upstart American Football League was battling established teams for draft picks. Initially perceived as something to be brushed aside like a mosquito, the AFL took hold and was ultimately taken on as an NFL partner in a merger, leading to the creation of the Super Bowl.

Despite his numerous contributions to the franchise over the long run, the selection of Mike Ditka as the number one pick in 1961 was perhaps Halas's greatest draft choice. However, a close reading of Halas's picks indicates that without the AFL competition, the 1963 Bears certainly would have been even greater. Among Bears selections were halfback Keith Lincoln and defensive tackle Ernie Ladd, terrific players who both signed instead with the San Diego Chargers. From the 1962 draft the Bears culled halfback Ronnie Bull and defensive end Ed O'Bradovich for the squad. In 1963, kicker Bob Jencks came aboard.

The 1963 Bears began the season with a 10–3 victory over the Packers. The win was a statement that they belonged with the

Draft Picks Gone Wrong

One reason the years after the 1963 championship were not kind to the Bears was mishandling of the annual player draft. Despite the selection of a couple of Hall of Famers, the Bears did not restock well.

Bears Number Ones, 1960–1970

1960—Roger Davis, G, Syracuse

1961—Mike Ditka, E, Pittsburgh

1962—Ronnie Bull, HB, Baylor

1963—Choice traded

1964—Dick Evey, T, Tennessee

1965—Dick Butkus, LB, Illinois; Gale Sayers, HB, Kansas; and Steve DeLong, T, Tennessee

1966—George Rice, T, LSU (never played for Bears)

1967—Loyd Phillips, DE, Arkansas

1968—Mike Hull, RB, USC

1969—Rufus Mayes, T, Ohio State

1970—Choice traded

best. In mid-November, the Bears topped the Packers again, this time 26–7. Sweeping the Packers in the early 1960s was no easy task.

No one can say that the Bears took an easy path to the championship. They left their brand name on the Packers' psyche, and they found themselves once again facing their favorite Eastern Division rival New York Giants for the crown. Fortunato said the city was in a frenzy about the Bears being back in the limelight. Fans hungered for a championship again and transferred their emotions to the team.

"Man, they were all hepped up about us playing that game," he said. "You just couldn't go anyplace to eat or anything. People would come around you and talk about the game, and they were all fired up. Everybody was really fired up going into that game, I'll tell you. I'm talking about the fans and everybody else."

This was a loaded Giants team, a club with one of the most explosive offenses in team history. The quarterback was Y. A. Tittle, the only man besides Sid Luckman to toss 7 touchdown passes in a single NFL game. His receiver of choice was the fleet Del Shofner. Key men in the New York backfield were Frank Gifford and Alex Webster. The Giants' defense, with such stalwarts as linebacker Sam Huff, defensive back Jimmy Patton, and linemen like Rosey Grier and Andy Robustelli, was nearly as intimidating as the Bears'. It was a pick-'em game when the teams lined up on a cold December 29 at Wrigley Field.

At the time Huff was the best-known defensive player in the sport. A television special called *The Violent World of Sam Huff* took fans inside the game and portrayed Huff as not only the best middle linebacker, but a ferocious tackler who made ball carriers

Bill George was the first of a long line of Chicago Bears star middle linebackers. He played for the Bears from 1952 to 1965.
George Brace Collection

quake. However, the Bears thought this was the New York hype machine whirling at top speed. Their vote for best middle linebacker went to Bill George, who after retirement was tragically killed in a vehicular accident.

"Bill George was as good a linebacker as there was in the NFL in the 1950s and 1960s," fullback Rick Casares said. "He absolutely got overshadowed by Huff, but he was a better football player than Huff. He was quicker and smarter."

Snow was plowed off the grass field beforehand, and when the players emerged from the locker rooms, their breath spiraled into the air as if they were exhaling cigaratte smoke. By this time, Halas was forty-three years into his pro career, and since so much time had elapsed since his previous championship, this younger generation of players wanted to provide a fresh title for him. Both O'Bradovich and Ditka spoke of winning the game for "The Old Man."

It was eleven degrees with an 11-mile-per-hour wind. The conditions mediated in favor of the Bears because, despite scoring 301 points in the regular season, Chicago was more prepared to make up any offensive power loss on defense. It is the defense that is remembered best from this Bears club. Whether that is because it was vastly superior to the offense, as Pettibon claimed, or it simply best fit the team image in Bears legend, it was huge on this day.

The crowd of 45,801 witnessed a defensive fight. There were no big offensive numbers in this game. Bull rushed for a team-leading 42 yards, and the Giants' top ground gainer was Joe Morrison with 61. No one on either team caught more than 3 passes. Tittle was stymied, throwing for just 147 yards with 11 comple-

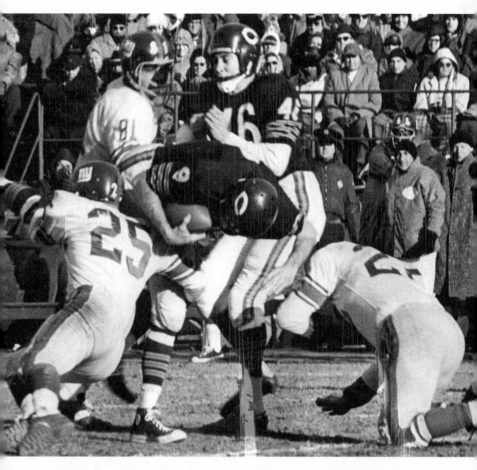

Bears quarterback Bill Wade (9) dives for a third-quarter first down during the team's 14–10 victory over the New York Giants in the 1963 NFL championship game. Chicago Tribune Archives

tions on 29 attempts. Bears signal-caller Bill Wade posted similar stats with 10 completions in 28 tries for 138 yards. Not much highlight material there.

However, Wade, a 6'2", 202-pound thrower out of Vanderbilt, who was appreciated as a leader more than as a flashy quarterback, scored touchdowns on runs of 2 yards and 1 yard. Both of his scores followed interceptions. The Bears demoralized the Giants by hounding Tittle into five interceptions.

In the first quarter, Tittle completed a 14-yard touchdown pass to Gifford, the former University of Southern California golden boy who went on to *Monday Night Football*–announcing renown. Before the fifteen-minute period ended, Wade put his first TD on the board. Kicker Don Chandler booted a 13-yard field goal in the second quarter to give the Giants a 10–7 halftime lead. But the Bears answered with Wade's second run in the third quarter, and that score held up for a 14–10 Chicago victory.

The underlying story was the pressure of the defensive linemen on Tittle and the take-turns interceptions scenario. Morris returned one for 61 yards to set up a Wade score. O'Bradovich (who set up Wade's other touchdown), Pettibon, Dave Whitsell, and Bennie McRae each gathered in an off-target Tittle pass.

Many of the players from that 1963 club retain a special bond, and several of them talk regularly on the telephone. "I'm gonna tell you why it was a special team," Fortunato said. "Because we had a lot of regular guys on that team. We didn't have any really big stars. We all played together, and we got along together.

"Our defense got along with our offense. We went out together, we did things together. We really had a lot of camaraderie. A lot of times teams don't have that, and we had that. We didn't have the best players, but I'll tell you what, we had players who gave us 110 percent and did a helluva job."

A Season Broken by Death

The Bears of 1963 were not built for a long run; they peaked at the right moment to win a championship. Yet no one expected the abrupt fall of the club. In one of the most dramatic tumbles in NFL history, the Bears went from world class to world-class flop.

Tragedy tainted the tight-knit team of the year before. The chemistry of a team and the intangibles that make it a winner are sometimes fragile, and the Bears who fell to a 5–9 record in 1964 were ruined by a real-world intrusion.

When the team assembled for training camp in Rensselaer, Indiana, that summer, the glow of the championship season had not yet worn off. Key players were back, and repeating was on everyone's mind. It was unthinkable that the Bears would not compete in another playoff game until 1977.

The Bears stayed in rooms at St. Joseph's College. After practice one evening, halfback Willie Galimore, a speedy, elusive runner with tremendous potential, and end John Farrington, both of whom started in the title game, went out for some relaxation and were on their way back to the school. Farrington, a four-year man out of Prairie View A&M, caught 21 passes for 2 touchdowns during the title season. Galimore, whose magnificent slashing ability was only approaching full bloom, rushed for 321 yards and 5 touchdowns.

With Galimore at the wheel, the Volkswagen Beetle swung out of control on a sharp curve, soared over a ditch, and rolled. Both players were killed. Farrington was thrown from the car, and Galimore suffered a broken neck inside the smashed car. That season was broken on the spot as well. The grieving Bears wore black armbands during games in order to honor their teammates. Showing his softer side, Halas paid for the educations of all three Galimore children.

That season the Bears griped about lack of financial bonuses they felt Halas had promised if they won the title, suffered several key injuries, and seemed not to recover from the pall cast by the deaths of two important teammates. Nothing was the same.

As a result of the poor 1964 finish, the Bears earned a high draft choice. Halas used it to select the spectacular Gale Sayers.

Stan Jones, who was later elected to the Hall of Fame, had the unusual distinction of being one of the last NFL players to shift back and forth between offensive guard and tackle and defensive tackle and started the championship game on defense. After a long assistant-coaching career, Jones lives in retirement in Colorado. He played at 6'1" and about 250 pounds, and by modern NFL standards, that makes him more of a midget than a lineman. He jokes that if he were playing today at that weight, he would be a cornerback.

Jones came into the league in 1954 from the University of Maryland, where he had played both ways. But by 1963 he was bored with blocking guys and relished the opportunity to play defensive tackle.

"I was a guard, and frankly, it got a little old," Jones said. "I was a pulling guard. On defense I was going after the ball, and it was different. I liked hitting guys. We were very good at it. On that defense we set all kinds of records. It had good people on it. We had a good group. One-hundred and forty-four points, that's pretty good."

Jones was a throwback, not only to the two-way players of the past. When he was inducted into the Hall of Fame in Canton, Ohio, in 1991, he did a lot more than say thanks a bunch to those who helped him along the way. He gave an old-school speech, urging the NFL to tamp down its reliance on specialization and return to the days of iron men and more hard-nosed play.

"Outlaw the mass substitution," Jones said. "Makes you half sick. Second and long everybody comes off the bench, everybody goes back on the bench. All the trick football, get rid of it. Bring back the days of grass surfaces and outdoor stadiums." Spoken like a true George Halas disciple.

The 1963 championship team—a special one for Bears fans who were not yet born when the squad swept through the 1940s—was built gradually through the 1950s. Linebacker Fortunato, who is in his 70s, said fans do seem to have long memories and still applaud the Bears of 1963. "You know," he said, "I have more requests for autographs, for appearances and this, that, and everything since I got old than I did when I was playing."

The 1956 run to the championship game, even though it was lost to the Giants, heralded the start of a fine Bears era. The year after the Bears lost Sneakers Game II, there was a great deal of preseason attention. One sports magazine featured Jones, Casares, and George on its cover with this message: THE MONSTERS OF THE MIDWAY ARE BACK.

Maybe the magazine was premature with the boldness of the pronouncement, but the Bears were on their way back, and the 1963 championship team put the exclamation point at the end of that story. That magazine piece was precious to Casares at the time, and he recalls it with fondness today. "I just loved it," he said. "It's a great article, and it's my favorite."

To any Bears player who competed under Halas, from the title teams of the 1920s and 1930s to the title teams of the 1940s, and who experienced the sweet victory of 1963, being called a Monster of the Midway was a special motto and was worn as a badge of honor.

The Kansas Comet

It is all on film, the way Gale Sayers darted, slashed, twisted, and left everyone in the mud, grasping for his ankles; and so it is not all talk, not all flickering memory when the old-timers make their case. You watch the legs stride and the body slither, and yes, you see what cannot be quantified, what cannot be explained by the rigidity of either mathematical equations or basic descriptions.

He is as fluid as water, but he could not be bottled. On the day the rookie from Kansas officially introduced himself to the National Football League, historians' superlatives froze in place. It took only games, only amounting to a few seasons, for those who watched with jaws dropping to proclaim Sayers one of the greatest running backs who ever lived.

And because of the brevity of it all, it is important that what Sayers did during the confines of one sixty-minute game is preserved, can be seen by those not yet born, can be witnessed by those not then in attendance.

Collector's item: film from the December 12, 1965, Chicago Bears game against the San Francisco 49ers. Final score, Chicago 61, San Francisco 20. On that rainy, muddy day, Gale Sayers scored 6 touchdowns. It is probably the most legendary single-game individual performance in Bears history. There were 46,278 paid witnesses, but who knows how many claim they were present in person under the slate gray sky at Wrigley Field?

It was nearing the end of Sayers's rookie year, and the 6'0", 198-pound runner was a known quantity by then. The 49ers, who beat the Bears by 28 points in the season opener (in which Sayers figured only in the "also played" category), understood the difference of a few months. The visitors devoted their pregame scheme entirely to shutting down Sayers. They actually called their formation the "Chicago defense."

Players of that time, like big Charlie Krueger and linebacker Matt Hazeltine, actually said that their coaches repeated "Sayers, Sayers, Sayers" all week in practice as if it was a magic spell.

The so-called "Chicago defense" was a strategy that failed as miserably as a forecast for a sun-splashed weekend obliterated by a hurricane. Oops. One reason the opposing coaches repeated Sayers's name in triplicate was that it seemed as if there were three of him. Sayers-number-one ran nine times for 113 yards for

4 touchdowns. Sayers-number-two caught 2 passes for 89 yards and 1 touchdown. Sayers-number-three ran back punts for 134 more yards and a sixth touchdown.

Six touchdowns. That equaled the National Football League record set by the legendary Ernie Nevers of the Chicago Cardinals in 1929 and tied by the Cleveland Browns' Dub Jones in 1951. Sayers did it in soaking-wet conditions, with every chance to slip and fall. He didn't boast afterwards but said simply of the 49ers defense, "I knew where I was going and they didn't."

Running back Gale Sayers on the loose in a 1971 exhibition game.
Chicago Tribune Archives

During that rookie season, Sayers scored a phenomenal 22 touchdowns. He was the latest, and fans thought he might be the greatest. And he might have been, if his knees had cooperated. Ultimately, crippling knee injuries reduced his speed and mobility and caused the gradual diminishment of his world-class ability. By 1971 he was retired. In college, Sayers had been dubbed the "Kansas Comet," but in outer space terminology he was more akin to a supernova that burned brightly but briefly.

Even today knee injuries can be devastating to athletes who rely on speed and slashing ability to succeed. In the 1960s a serious knee injury like the one initially inflicted on Sayers's right knee was often career ending. At the least, it was assumed that a running back would never be the same.

When Sayers suffered his first knee injury, George Halas, the tough old bird who had survived on grit in the league for decades, said he cried along with the player—hurt not as much because of the talent at risk but because of the type of human being harmed.

There is little doubt that Sayers's injuries were an athletic catastrophe. His eruption upon the scene, exploding from the Bears backfield, heralded the coming of something new, something fresh, in a sense a technological advancement for the NFL. Sayers was a forerunner of the great backs to follow, the likes of O. J. Simpson and Barry Sanders. Yet it was as if an astronomer looked up in the sky one night and discovered a new star blinking at him, then a month later looked again and the star was missing. He would be forever haunted, seeking to sort out what he truly saw.

Sayers grew up in Omaha, Nebraska, and was considered a traitor for choosing Kansas over the University of Nebraska. By the time he was taken as a first-round draft pick, the Bears knew what they were getting in the two-time All-American. Early on, Ed McCaskey, a team official who was Halas's daughter Virginia's husband, dubbed Sayers "Black Magic." Sayers liked the nickname.

Sayers was the Bears' top pick (along with Dick Butkus) in 1965, and he was not particularly intimidated by gruff team leader Halas. From the start, Sayers said, Halas gave him good advice about how to lead his life off the field and how to build a career that would carry him beyond football. "I'm glad I played for a man like George Halas," Sayers said.

Sayers was one of Halas's favorites, not only a player whose skill he admired but who he sensed was a good person with a good future. "I've never seen anyone run with Gale's agility," Halas said early in the runner's career.

That was it. Sayers was hard to catch, hard to pin down, and his movements were so smooth they were like tall grass swaying in the wind. His style was exhilarating. He squirted through holes that didn't seem to be there and slashed past outstretched arms. It was a gift born of instinct and speed.

Some say that if Halas hadn't taken Sayers out before the end of his 6-touchdown game, he would have gone right on scoring touchdowns that day. Maybe even 8 touchdowns, a number that would have put the record over the rainbow. Sayers has never worried about that. He said that at the time he had no idea that 6 touchdowns in a single game was even the record.

"We didn't think about records back then," Sayers said four decades later. "I didn't think about records. You know, I figured that once we got ahead, 30 points, or whatever the score was, I was coming out, and that's what happened. Usually, you bring in the second string and let them play some. You bring in the third string and let them play some. But, you know, today everybody's got record books ready on the sidelines. 'Oh, he needs another fumble to break this record, or he needs to do this or do that.' We didn't care about records. We wanted to win the ball game and get everybody in the game and give them a chance to play."

What made Sayers so spectacular was his versatility. He took handoffs and ran from scrimmage, he caught passes, and he was electrifying in the open field returning punts. Sayers rushed for a career-high 1,231 yards his second season and for 1,032 yards in 1969, leading the league in rushing both times when it was a fourteen-game schedule. But he was sort of like one of those James Bond movie weapons that starts out as an innocent can opener, becomes a deadly knife, can be transformed into a silencer pistol, and before you know it morphs into a machine gun. Sayers was certainly a multipurpose weapon, and that's what set him apart. Once in a while he also threw a touchdown pass on the halfback option.

After watching the prodigy up close for some time, Halas called Sayers the best running back of all time, with more talent than anyone. "He also had more bad luck and more injuries, too," Halas said.

Sayers had never suffered a major injury until the right knee gave way and did not know how to cope with the wound that affected his psyche as much as his body. Already a shy individual, Sayers became depressed and withdrawn while rehabbing. In his autobiography, I Am Third, Sayers confessed to a self-doubt he had never felt before.

Supreme athletes possess supreme confidence, and they consider themselves invulnerable—until something like a severe knee injury alters the playing field. Sayers said the right knee injury involved the tearing of all ligaments on the inner side of the knee, plus a torn anterior cruciate ligament. At first he refused to believe his doctor that surgery would bring him back to full strength. It did, but not without struggle, and later injuries eventually brought him down.

For all of the frustration, disappointment, and might-have-beens that trailed Sayers, limiting him to less than four full, healthy, productive running seasons in pro football, he is as much identified and remembered by a certain segment of the public for his relationship with Brian Piccolo.

When Sayers emerged from college and joined the Bears in 1965, the United States was in turmoil. The civil rights movement accounted for much of the front-page news. Although he did not define himself as militant, Sayers had participated in demonstrations on campus. There was as much consciousness about race in American society in the 1960s as there had been at any time since the Civil War.

With that backdrop, Halas chose to put together as road roommates Sayers, a black from the Great Plains, and Piccolo, a back from Florida who played at Wake Forest and joined the Bears as a free agent the year after Sayers. Both men were accepting but wary at first. Then they and their spouses became great friends. The black-and-white mix was unheard of in professional sports at the time.

Halas said he matched the two running backs because Sayers was reserved and quiet and Piccolo was outgoing and had charisma, and he hoped some of Piccolo would rub off on Sayers. He also said he felt they were extraordinary people who could handle any pressure or garbage thrown their way because of the black-white arrangement.

Brian's Song: Beautiful Music Together

Gale Sayers and Brian Piccolo were surprised when Bears coach George Halas suggested in 1967 that the two running backs room together on the road, because Sayers was black and Piccolo was white. No such arrangement previously had been known to occur in major professional team sports.

Brian Piccolo died tragically of cancer in his twenties. The movie Brian's Song tells the story of his friendship with teammate Gale Sayers. Chicago Tribune Archives

They became friends, and at a time of unrest across the country, they were symbols of how blacks and whites could learn to live together. Sayers never had a close relationship with a white person before sharing a room with Piccolo. Piccolo was seen in some quarters as a son of the South because he attended Wake Forest, although he had been born in Massachusetts and attended high school in Fort Lauderdale, Florida.

Piccolo led the nation in scoring (111 points) and rushing (1,044 yards) while in college but was a second-option back in the pros. His best year was 1968, when he ran for 450 yards. He was known for his sense of humor and for working hard in practice, though nobody outside of the team and family members would have known it if producers had not decided to seize upon the idea of Piccolo and Sayers's relationship and Piccolo's tragic death from cancer as a TV movie topic.

Brian's Song aired on ABC in 1971 and starred Billy Dee Williams as Sayers (he was nominated for an Emmy award) and James Caan as Piccolo. The picture won an Emmy for best feature-length program and in all garnered eleven Emmy nominations. The viewing audience was huge, and the attention it received was also intense because of both the subject matter and its emotional power. *Brian's Song* was also one of the first made-for-TV movies.

Despite the movie's popularity and its enduring legacy as a film that can make even men cry, the picture was remade and shown in December 2001. The remake expanded the original from seventy-three minutes to eighty-nine and included additional footage built around Piccolo's best friend Ralph Kurek, a lesser-known Bears player, and the wives of the protagonists.

The original movie was well received, but a book written by Jeannie Morris, a former Chicago television reporter who was married to ex-Bears receiver Johnny Morris, is considered more authoritative and detailed in its account of what truly happened in 1969 and 1970. The book is entitled *Brian Piccolo: A Short Season.*

No one could imagine that the partnership begun so simply as travel roommates would become the most famous friendship in American sports history. Halas could not foresee how extraordinary the groundbreaking pairing would become and not because of the black and white of the men's skins.

Yes, the players did thrive, come to appreciate one another, and enjoy a friendship that transcended both the playing field and the hotel room. But their relationship comes to mind today because of sadness and tragedy. Piccolo developed a persistent cough during the 1969 season and, when he had doctors check it out, was diagnosed with a tumor in his chest the size of a grapefruit.

A four-and-a-half-hour surgery removed the tumor and provided hope for Piccolo's recovery. But he relapsed, endured more surgeries, and died from cancer at age twenty-six. Sayers was still an active player when he wrote *I Am Third*, and the story of his connection to Brian Piccolo was only one chapter. But the chapter was expanded into the television movie *Brian's Song* that was a hit in the early 1970s and is regarded as a classic now. The story touched Americans on many levels, from those who enjoyed the byplay between the two young men and considered it a positive parable for race relations to those moved to tears by the demise of an athlete stricken young.

Sayers's football career ended too soon. But later he had success as an athletic administrator at his alma mater and as athletic director at Southern Illinois University, and he became a successful businessman after settling in the Chicago area.

Sayers also became the youngest player ever inducted into the Pro Football Hall of Fame in 1977. Sayers, like only a handful of others such as Sid Luckman and Mike Ditka, was family to

The Brian Piccolo Award

To honor Brian Piccolo's memory, Bears veterans present an annual award to the player "who best exemplifies the courage, loyalty, teamwork, dedication and sense of humor" of the late running back. Initially, the award was given only to rookies. In 1992, it was expanded to include veterans. Here are the winners through 2004:

1970 Glen Holloway; 1971 Jerry Moore; 1972 Jim Osborne; 1973 Wally Chambers; 1974 Fred Pagac; 1975 Roland Harper; 1976 Brian Bashnagel; 1977 Ted Albrecht; 1978 John Skibinski; 1979 Dan Hampton.

1980 Bob Fisher; 1981 Mike Singletary; 1982 Jim McMahon; 1983 Jim Covert; 1984 Shaun Gayle; 1985 Kevin Butler; 1986 Neal Anderson; 1987 Ron Morris; 1988 James Thornton and Mickey Pruitt; 1989 Trace Armstrong.

1990 Mark Carrier; 1991 Chris Zorich; 1992 Mike Singletary and Troy Auzenne; 1993 Tom Waddle, Myron Baker, and Todd Perry; 1994 Shaun Gayle and Raymont Harris; 1995 Erik Kramer and Rashaan Salaam; 1996 Chris Zorich and Bobby Engram; 1997 Ryan Enright, John Allred, and Van Hiles; 1998 Bobby Engram and Tony Parrish; 1999 Marcus Robinson and Jerry Azumah.

2000 Clyde Simmons and Brian Urlacher; 2001 James Williams and Anthony Thomas; 2002 Phillip Daniels and Alex Brown; 2003 Olin Kreutz and Charles Tillman; 2004 Olin Kreutz and Tommie Harris.

George Halas—another son, the youngest son in Papa Bear's long career. The Bears team founder was asked to be Sayers's presenter at the ceremonies in Canton, Ohio. Halas wrote in his autobiography, "I did so, with love and joy."

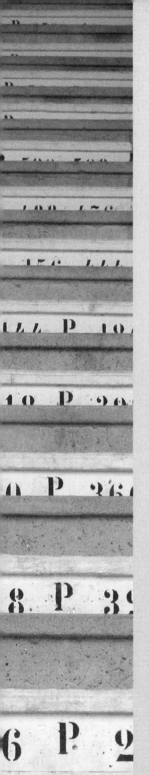

An Old New Home

Many young fans, whose memories do not stretch back to Elvis Presley, grow up believing that Soldier Field has always been the home of Chicago Bears football. If someone notes in their presence that Wrigley Field was the home of the Bears for fifty years, much longer than Soldier Field, the reaction is most commonly, "Really?"

Soldier Field did not become the Bears' home playground until 1971, and the version of Soldier Field now looming over the shore of Lake Michigan in downtown Chicago has only been in use since 2003.

The stadium was conceived in 1919 as a memorial to the more than 120,000 American armed-services personnel killed during World War I. Soldier Field opened in 1924, and Notre Dame and Northwestern played the first football game there on November 22. At the time the building was known as Municipal Grant Park Stadium and held 45,000 fans. By the late 1920s, when the stadium had adopted its current name, Soldier Field had been expanded to hold more than 100,000 fans. Soon it was hosting 123,000 spectators for a Notre Dame–Southern Cal football game and in 1927 was the site of the Jack Dempsey–Gene Tunney heavyweight championship fight.

Wrigley Days

Between 1922 and 1970, the Chicago Bears played 332 games at Wrigley Field, home of the baseball-playing Chicago Cubs, compiling a record of 221–89–22 at the old ballyard.

Also, due to special circumstances, the Bears hosted a handful of games around Chicago at stadiums besides Wrigley and Soldier Fields. In 1925 the Bears won a home game at DePaul University. In 1931 the Bears won a home game at Loyola University. And during the renovation of Soldier Field in 2002, the Bears played eight home games at the University of Illinois Memorial Stadium, finishing 3–5.

One of the architectural trademarks of Soldier Field was its rows of colonnades, which gave it a distinguished, readily identifiable old-style Greek-inspired construction appearance. No cookie-cutter circular stadium for the Bears. Such stadiums were going up all over the place in the early 1970s and were home to teams like the Philadelphia Eagles at Veterans Stadium and the Pittsburgh Steelers in Three Rivers Stadium.

George Halas, whose stewardship of the Bears predated the existence of Soldier Field, presided over the switch from Wrigley, which became the exclusive province of the Cubs baseball team, to the bigger home perched over the deep blue waters of Lake Michigan. To the Bears, it was a place of their own.

Despite all of the history written at Wrigley, the Bears and Soldier Field seemed the perfect match. Although it can always be classified as hyperbole when pro football and real war are mentioned in the same sentence, the comparison between going to war on the gridiron and going to war in the trenches is often made. And over the years, it had been ingrained in fans' minds that the team was always one of the toughest in the NFL, so it made a certain amount of sense to play in a stadium that paid homage to war dead.

The Bears, with their Monsters of the Midway persona, were a fitting representative for a city that prided itself on hard work and withstanding rugged winters and that possessed a willingness to get down and dirty. A tough town and a tough team. The dual image goes together perfectly.

"Yes, it does," said Rick Casares, the 1950s–1960s-era Bears fullback who grew up in Florida and New York. "And it's a great image. I've always thought of the New York Yankees as baseball and the Chicago Bears as professional football. I grew up following them and idolizing them."

Soldier Field had Dempsey and Tunney, and from 1971 on it has had the Bears. The only problem was that the dynamics of pro football marketing changed, and Soldier Field lacked luxury boxes for high-roller season ticketholders. That lack grew to be viewed as more acute in the 1990s. At the same time, the concrete stadium was aging; the Bears wanted a new stadium. Just where such a playing field would be placed and who would pay for it occupied the attention of everyone from Mayor Richard M. Daley to the McCaskey family, operators of the team over the nearly twenty years since Halas's death in 1983. After massive lobbying, intricate planning, and intense arguing, a plan was hatched to renovate Soldier Field.

The complex idea aimed to preserve some of the best features of the old stadium while modernizing the rest of it with the amenities NFL fans of today expect. There was a great hullabaloo over what to keep from the old stadium, what to add (more restrooms!), and how to maintain the dignity of the old stadium and its purpose of honoring casualties of war.

Complicating the issue was the impossibility of renovating Soldier Field during one off-season. There just wasn't enough time to transform the grand old structure between January and September. To undertake the $632 million project, the Bears had to abandon their home field for one season. Arrangements were made to play home games during the 2002 season at the University of Illinois Memorial Stadium in Champaign, roughly 150 miles south of Chicago. There was a certain symmetrical appropriateness in the location. After all, that's where Red Grange first

Soldier Field was renovated to give it a modern interior with numerous amenities while preserving the famous columns on the exterior. Chicago Tribune Archives

made a name for himself and where Halas got his college degree.

Even with the pressure eased somewhat by borrowing the Fighting Illinis' stadium, every available minute was needed to complete Soldier Field for the start of the 2003 season. The Bears threw a wrench into the plans when they finished 13–3 in the 2001 regular season and advanced to the playoffs. The builders had counted on the Bears playing a nondescript season, certainly not claiming the Central Division title under coach-of-the-year Dick Jauron.

By the time the Bears' season ended with a 33–19 playoff loss to the Eagles, it was January 19. Reporters in the press box were astonished to see the field torn up before their eyes. Less than an hour after fans vacated, demolition began. Late departers from the game were forced to leave through an alternate exit and had to weave in and out of heavy equipment. The message was clear: Every second counted.

The Bears' season in Champaign was a strange one. Jauron kept telling players and sportswriters that heading to the central part of the state, spending a night in a hotel room before the game, and then taking a long trip home made no difference.

However, early in the season players complained about their accommodations, causing a shift to a new team hotel. The eight regular-season Bears home games created more traffic in Champaign and brought business to hotels and restaurants—but only in short bursts, since neither the team nor the out-of-town fans lingered. Realistic Bears players opined that the season would be like playing all road games.

With hopes high after the 2001 success, the Bears unraveled during 2002, finishing 4–12. It was difficult to blame the commute to Champaign or homesickness for Soldier Field. Too many things went wrong. The absence of Soldier Field from the Bears' life was probably just coincidence.

Work on a new-look Soldier Field progressed steadily (court challenges to the project were fought off) while the Bears were on their season-long road trip. The construction project was out of the limelight most of the time. Most drivers—especially early

The meshing of the old and new made architectural critics and others apoplectic, but ticket holders loved the new sight lines inside the stadium.
Chicago Tribune Archives

on—passing nearby in typical heavy city traffic could not tell exactly what was going on. Their views revealed cranes, concrete columns, and the shell of an interior, but they really couldn't picture how things were coming together.

One observer who made it a point to both study the plans and listen to those who took a close look and did not like what they saw was Pulitzer Prize–winning *Chicago Tribune* architecture critic Blair Kamin. He thought the entire venture misguided. Early comments fielded from irate observers indicated deep feelings of outrage and produced descriptions of the coming stadium as an "abomination" and a "mistake by the lake."

The Meanest Monster of Them All

During the 2005 football season, an ad running on the radio to promote Reebok athletic shoes featured Dick Butkus, the once-ferocious linebacker of the Chicago Bears, parodying his meanness on the field. In the commercial Butkus said it was too bad the NFL didn't have a sportsmanship award when he was playing because he would have won it every year. When the announcer scoffed, asking about all of those vicious hits Butkus committed between 1965 and 1973, Butkus replied that they were hugs.

Hugs? Sure, if a life-and-death struggle with a grizzly is a waltz. No one who shared a football field with the 6'3", 245-pound Butkus during his college days at Illinois or during his pro days with the Bears, ever accused him of being huggable. Many accused him of being the greatest middle linebacker of all time and perhaps the toughest, most hard-nosed football player in history.

When Butkus tackled you, you stayed down. He had the speed to track running backs across the field as if the ball tucked under their arms was a homing device. He had the power to duel large, muscular linemen. And he had the heart and desire to play hard when his knees were gimpy.

Butkus, who grew up on the south side of Chicago, missed the Bears championship of 1963. He was drafted in 1965, draft pick number 1A to Gale Sayers's number 1B. Now that was a draft. The two Bears greats were linked forevermore. They were the cornerstones of the defense and offense. They were supposed to return a title to Chitown, but both of them had their careers stunted by severe knee injuries. In 1994, the Bears retired their playing numbers together, Butkus's 51 and Sayers's 40.

Butkus was chosen for the all–National Football League team seven times during his nine-year career and built a reputation as a no-mercy defender who hit so hard he would rattle your teeth and jar your bones. Much like Sayers's career, Butkus's was frustrating because of injuries and left historians exclaiming about what might have been.

Middle linebacker Dick Butkus was often called the meanest man in football during his 1965–73 career. George Brace Collection

Butkus coauthored an autobiography with writer Pat Smith, entitled *Flesh and Blood: How I Played the Game,* that came out in 1997. A passage in the book reveals some of the depth of his commitment to football. "People say that I had a great tolerance for pain," Butkus wrote. "Since I have never lived inside another player's body, I have no idea if that is true. But I do know that I wanted to play football better than anyone else, and perhaps that explains why I was able to push the pain down, lock it in until the game was over."

The way Butkus played the game full speed ahead, and the way he hit opposing ball carriers on his way to a 1979 Hall of Fame induction, he dished out his own hefty share of pain.

Kamin warned early on that the revamping of Soldier Field might be viewed as tampering by some. Soldier Field had been named a National Historic Landmark in 1987; it was one of just 2,341 listed at the time of the new construction. He suggested the city was risking the loss of the stadium's designation as historically significant. The National Park Service had already put city officials on notice that it felt the basic architectural integrity of the stadium might be irretrievably changed by the renovation.

A year before Soldier Field reopened, Kamin wrote, "Looking at the stadium from the north and south, one could easily conclude that it has been invaded by a lopsided UFO." Not the most flattering description for a landmark structure going up on the lakefront that was supposed to be a milestone.

Work continued. Chicagoans were nervous, and when the stadium opened on September 29, 2003, for a Bears–Green Bay Packers game, reviews were mixed. Those who hated the idea of overlapping the gleaming silvery bowl of a field inside the old, existing colonnades hated the real thing. Those like Kamin who had sarcastically referred to the exterior as resembling a spaceship could not be refuted.

The week before Soldier Field reopened for football, Kamin weighed in with a tome analyzing every aspect of the place. If Soldier Field were a movie, Kamin's review probably would have been one-and-a-half stars. "The new Soldier Field, the face that launched a thousand quips, is almost here," he wrote. "A skillful, sometimes brilliant and ultimately jarring failure." He termed the mix of styles "Klingon meets Parthenon, an architectural close encounter of the worst kind."

However, the interior, Kamin noted, was a veritable "pigskin palace." Fans agreed. Those who bought season tickets, who were among the 61,500 fans the renovated stadium now seated, inhabited a different world from the critics. They were not on the outside looking up at an alien vessel. They were on the inside, looking down at a football game, and they had marvelous sight lines. If gripes about the architecture were many, never was a complaint heard from those watching the games. The new Soldier Field might have irked the National Park Service, but it was a good place to watch a game. No complaints were uttered by coaches or players about the facility, either.

A year after the stadium reopened, a special ceremony was held to commemorate an addition. A 26½-foot-tall granite bas-relief sculpture featuring Bears legends—most prominently Halas—was unveiled in a concourse. The artistic work—which weighs 11,500 pounds—honored Halas, Red Grange, Bronko Nagurski, Sid Luckman, Bill George, Mike Singletary, and Walter Payton for their places in Bears history.

Bears Hall of Fame linebacker Dick Butkus looked over the sculpture, studied the picture of Halas, and proclaimed it accurate. "It's right on the mark," Butkus said of the depiction of Halas. "It looks like he is yelling at people. That's what he did."

Super

It was *Animal House* in cleats, the circus on the gridiron. The players made 'em laugh, and the football made 'em gasp.

Some say the 1985 Chicago Bears were the greatest football team in National Football League history. At the least, they are on the short list. The 1986 Super Bowl champions left Chicago with its best football memories ever and treated fans nationwide to the greatest show on earth. Send in the clowns, indeed. Crack the whip for the dangerous animals.

The 1985 season was the growl heard around the world. It was Mike Ditka breathing fire, a defensive unit crunching bones, William "The Refrigerator" Perry flattening would-be tacklers and would-be blockers, and

Walter Payton meshing his penchant for practical jokes with the purest dignity on the team.

It seems unfathomable that more than two decades have passed since the heyday of the world champions. In Chicago the memory is as fresh as yesterday. So many of the ex-Bears settled in the Windy City area that they are ubiquitous each autumn. You can't turn on the radio or TV without hearing or seeing what the Bears of the past think about the Bears of the present. And so admired and honored do they remain by the fans who lived through the fun and games that for the twentieth-anniversary season of the victory, the team participated in event after event and even incorporated to share profits from reunion appearances and commemorative keepsakes.

Feeling his own mortality in 1982 at the beginning of the illness that would eventually kill him, George Halas handpicked Mike Ditka to be the next coach of the Bears. Halas chose wisely. Ditka was as passionate and determined as a coach as he had been as a player. He was the hardcore Bear of Halas's dreams when he became a Hall of Fame tight end. He bled Bears orange and blue, and he expected his players to honor the legacy Halas had built and left behind. Ditka ate nails instead of pretzels for snacks. He yelled first and asked questions later. He hated to lose, and whoever got in the way, well, they should have gotten out of the way. When a *Sports Illustrated* poll of 200 NFL players was taken in 1985, Ditka tied with Don Shula as the coach players would least like to play for. Ditka said he was "flattered" and said, "They're probably lazy butts who wouldn't want to pay the price."

The 1984 Bears started it. They finished 10–6, and the promise was evident, especially when they defeated the Redskins,

Bears coach Mike Ditka, arms folded, keeps an eye on the field during a November 1985 game against the archrival Green Bay Packers. Chicago Tribune Archives

23–19, in Washington in the first round of the playoffs. It was a confidence-building triumph and a herald. The players knew then that they had the potential to be something special.

Ditka could sense it, too. He wanted to squeeze every last ounce of juice out of his players. That's how *he* played the game, and that's how he felt it should be played. He also knew the Bears had the talent to go far, that 1985 could be their year. Ditka was on television so much that season, prowling the sidelines, grimacing, screaming at players, that he might as well have had his own sitcom.

Emory Moorehead, the main tight end on the Super Bowl team, said Ditka drove them to succeed. "When you have a guy like that, I think football is all about the pressure and the fear of failure and the fear of being criticized," Moorehead said. "Ditka knew one way, and that was the fear of your job. If you don't do it, you're out. And that's what he'd tell you every week. If you don't do it, I'll find somebody else to do it. And the fear of losing your job and the ability to support your family really got players to play."

The Bears of 1985 won their first twelve games, setting a pattern for the season with a dominating defense supervised by defensive coordinator Buddy Ryan and with an opportunistic offense that featured halfback Walter Payton but took its cues from the flamboyant personality of Jim McMahon.

The defense's fearsome nature is best remembered. That unit allowed only 198 points and permitted only 37 fourth-quarter points all season. But the offense scored an impressive 456 points to lead the league. That unit was comparatively overlooked, but it was as powerful as a souped-up bulldozer.

There is little doubt that the defense of Richard Dent, Mike Singletary, Steve McMichael, and Gary Fencik was the signature half of the team. But most fans would be surprised to learn just how balanced the team's achievements were.

"You know," said center Jay Hilgenberg, a cornerstone of the offensive line, "football is the ultimate team game, and you're not going to have the number one defense in the league with an

Walter Payton played a key role in the Bears offense during the team's journey to Super Bowl XX.
Chicago Tribune Archives

offense that goes three and out all the time. It's a team game."

Yet Hilgenberg acknowledges that the defense implanted itself in the public's mind. "Offensive line coach Dick Stanfel, who is the best line coach in the NFL, had always communicated to us and expressed to us the night before a game that we had to understand when we won this game that the praise was going to go to other places," Hilgenberg said. "If we lost, the blame was going to come at us. So we knew what was going on all those games."

What was going on that fall was overwhelming for the rest of the league. Win number eleven was 44–0 over the Dallas Cowboys. Ditka called the destruction of the Cowboys, then known as "America's Team," "awesome." The Bears had not beaten Dallas since 1971, and Ditka had played for the Cowboys and apprenticed as an assistant coach under Tom Landry. His Bears knew how much he wanted the victory. "It seemed like the energy and electricity from him just flowed into the other players," Walter Payton said. "This one was for Mike."

Win number twelve was 36–0 over the Atlanta Falcons. By then, the Bears were certain they were going to run the table. Only they didn't. The next week they lost to the Miami Dolphins, 38–24. The Dolphins took pride in shutting down the Bears' streak, especially since Miami was the only team to go 17–0 on a Super Bowl run. The Bears probably should have won, but they had their one lapse. The Bears were angry when they failed.

Hall of Fame middle linebacker Mike Singletary was a stalwart of the Bears defense in the mid-1980s when the team won the Super Bowl. Chicago Tribune Archives

"You can't imagine how upset Ditka and everybody else was that we didn't win that game and win all of them," said Keith Van Horne, the right tackle on the Super Bowl club. "But on the other hand, I look at it as that got us refocused and made sure we were going to win the whole damned thing.

"That was the game Buddy and Ditka are going at it in the locker room at halftime. You've got Buddy blitzing the hell out of them while they're throwing the hell out of the ball at us. You've got Mike Ditka throwing the ball when I think Miami was one of the lowest ranked defenses to run against. The defense was in its regular game plan, but it wasn't the right thing. The halftime thing was going on, and that's not a good indication the team is going to win the game, you know." Afterwards, a defiant Ditka said, "Nobody has beat us yet. We beat ourselves."

The Miami game was the blip in the season. The Bears won their last three regular-season games to finish 15–1. By that time unaligned football fans around the country were as deeply in love with the Bears as Chicago fans. One reason was *The Super Bowl Shuffle*, the rap-style video recorded by several team members before the Super Bowl. It was the ultimate in arrogance, appropriately befitting a team that seemed invincible on paper and carried an air of invulnerability into games.

And then there was The Fridge. William Perry's weight was listed at 310 pounds. At the time, the history of 300-pounders in the NFL was limited. Gene "Big Daddy" Lipscomb played up his scowl. Ernie Ladd terrorized the American Football League. Bubba Smith had a broad smile and spoke in wry parables about breaking quarterbacks like wishbones. But The Fridge had more personality than all of those defensive behemoths combined.

The Super Bowl Shuffle

Of all the wacky stuff that occurred during the 1985 Bears run to Super Bowl XX, of all the offbeat side issues that astonished the fans and endeared a personality-rich football team to the public, the making of *The Super Bowl Shuffle* topped everything.

What football team makes a tongue-in-cheek singing-and-dancing video before it even captures a championship? Heck, what football team makes a singing-and-dancing video ever?

Da answer: Da Bears. Da Bears, the succinct, accented description of the team emanating from the mouths of the Super Fans during a skit on the television show *Saturday Night Live,* has attached itself to the Chicago football team evermore. It is now part of the lexicon of the team, as much an official title as "The Bears." When Chicagoans converse, the expression still brings a chuckle from fans.

Quarterback Jim McMahon appeared on the cover of *Rolling Stone.* William "Refrigerator" Perry made the masses laugh when he flashed his gap-toothed smile and tucked the pigskin into his belly and rumbled his 310-pound body into the line of scrimmage.

But nothing garnered a smidgeon of the attention of the so-called "Bears Shufflin' Crew," which recorded *The Super Bowl Shuffle.* Players from Walter Payton to Willie Gault, from Mike Singletary to Richard Dent, from McMahon to the Fridge, from Gary Fencik to Otis Wilson, Mike Richardson, and Steve Fuller each mouthed a verse.

The video was officially written by Richard E. Meyer and Melvin Owens, with music by Bobby Daniels and Lloyd Barry, all done in fun; some have also credited Dent and Perry for being wordsmiths. Regardless, no one could have imagined that the song performed as rap would become a wild sensation. Some said the Bears had rock-star status because of their 15–1 regular-season record and their mix of colorful players, but the *Shuffle* solidified it.

There had never been anything like it in sports entertainment. *The Super Bowl Shuffle* was nominated for a 1986 Grammy award in the category of Best Rhythm and Blues Vocal Performance but lost to Prince and the Revolution's "Kiss."

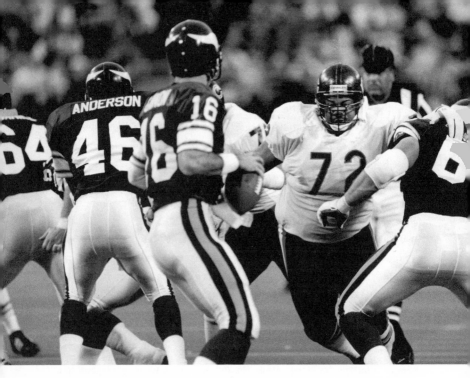

William "The Refrigerator" Perry (72) played on both sides of the ball during the Super Bowl season of 1985–86. *Chicago Tribune Archives*

He had a super nickname, and Ditka, perhaps initially to pay back the San Francisco 49ers for a perceived insult the year before when they ran 280-pound Guy McIntyre, had the brainstorm to use Perry as a first-down and goal-line running back.

"They ran a big, fat offensive guard in the backfield against us last year," defensive end Dan Hampton said after the game. "We thought we'd run a big, fat defensive lineman against them." Perry got a chuckle out of his new role. "When I got up from the pile, and the 49ers saw that I was the ball carrier," he said, "their eyes got real big."

Ryan didn't use Perry much on defense, so Ditka borrowed him. When the part-time job turned The Fridge into a sensation, making him the best-known appliance in the United States, Ditka kept it up. Perry even caught a touchdown pass against the Packers. Mr. Versatility.

It was casting against type. A big, strong, supposedly slow lineman carrying the ball and cracking jokes about his role. Perry was more athletic than the casual fan realized. Ditka insists that the big man, who later in his career escalated to around 350 pounds, provoking complaints from Ditka, played at 310 to 314 in 1985. In his book *In Life, First You Kick Ass*, Ditka said Perry was "a swizzle stick" that season. Even today, appearances in Chicago, or just the image of Perry coming to mind, or on television, brings a smile to Bears fans' faces.

The Bears were the main event and a sideshow all at once. Defensive end Richard Dent plowed through blockers for 17 sacks. Wide receiver Willie Gault, a onetime track star, ran a kick back 99 yards for a touchdown. Payton rushed for 1,551 yards and led the team in receptions with 49.

McMahon did not necessarily record magnificent, make-other-quarterbacks-envious stats. All he did was win, healthy or injured. He pulled out a Minnesota contest after not practicing all week and pleading to be inserted in the game. And then he played as hard as he worked. He was chastised by the league for writing messages on his headband. In New Orleans, at the Super Bowl, he mooned a passing helicopter.

The Bears were at their finest in the playoffs. In the first round they crushed the New York Giants, 21–0. This included the famous play when heavily rushed Giants punter Sean Landeta whiffed on a punt near his own end zone. In the second round, Chicago crushed the Los Angeles Rams, 24–0, in a game that ended in snow and high winds. Regardless of the circumstances, the Bears were just too good.

"To paraphrase Mike Ditka, we basically had a good team last year [1984], but second best wasn't good enough," said free safety Gary Fencik. "[He] really convinced everyone on both sides of the football we had the chance to get to the Super Bowl."

Fencik said defensive coordinator Buddy Ryan wrote out a plan each Friday informing defenders what it would take for them to win. "I have this sheet in my office that Buddy Ryan would write in a kind of quick summary of what we had to do to be successful," Fencik said. "It was pretty amazing. If you look at what he wrote for the New York Giants and the Los Angeles Rams, it was almost prescient what he said we had to do and what we were able to accomplish. In that Friday summary he would instill in you that swagger that this was a great team and you had to earn it, but if we played the way we practiced and according to the game plan, nobody could beat us. We became invincible after a while."

In the locker room before the Super Bowl game against New England, Buddy Ryan gave a valedictory address with tears in his eyes, telling the defense how much he loved them. The rumors had swirled that Ryan would accept the head coaching job with the Philadelphia Eagles, and the players understood he was gone.

When Ryan left the room, the demonstrable McMichael picked up a chair in anger and heaved it at the chalkboard. Stunningly, all four legs pierced the board and stuck there. Between the two segments of theater, one verbal, one action-packed, it was some pregame pep talk.

Gary Fencik, one of the stars of the 1985 Super Bowl team, waves to fans after a 1988 game at Soldier Field. Chicago Tribune Archives

Except for the Patriots' quick-strike field goal in the first quarter and a garbage-time touchdown in the fourth, the Bears were virtually in another solar system in their 46–10 Super Bowl victory. The only sour note was that Ditka rode his oversized actor Perry perhaps one play too many, allowing The Fridge to score on a 1-yard run instead of handing the ball to Payton. Payton deserved the opportunity for his achievements and class. Sometime after, Ditka said he regretted that choice.

On a freezing day in Chicago a few days after the January 26 Super Bowl triumph, the Bears were feted in a parade by 500,000 citizens lining the streets. It seemed as if the party would last forever, but it didn't even last another year. Ryan left for the Eagles, and although the Bears went 14–2, they did not repeat as Super Bowl champs.

Still, the Bears and Ditka got a pass in Chicago for a while. The great Super Bowl champs not only won it all, they did it with a style that a cold-weather, old-school town like Chicago appreciated.

"The image used to be the black-and-blue division and Monsters of the Midway," Moorehead said. "The Bears and Ditka brought all of that back. Everybody had a sense that 'We are the Bears' and 'We are the Central Division. It's going to be tough, and it's going to be rough, and we're going to mix it up with anybody, and we're not going to lose the battle. We're going to out-tough everybody.'

"The funny thing about playing football is that you take on the image of the coach, and we took on the image of the coach. I mean everybody was smoking cigars because the coach smoked cigars. You kind of emulate the coach. We had lost nine out of ten to Minnesota, I think, and he said, 'You know what? This is going to end.' You have to beat the Packers. We were able to control the division."

The Bears slipped and finished 5–11 in 1992, and in January of 1993, after eleven seasons as boss of the team, Ditka was fired.

Crunchers of the Midway

Almost from the moment the Bears clobbered the New England Patriots in the Super Bowl, it became the rage to hire a player to sell your product—and by all indications it is still a good investment.

Even the team media guide, normally known only for its statistical value, carried intriguing advertisements in the season following the championship. The inside back page featured a generic black-and-white sketch of a Bears player with a variety of corn-chip and potato-chip packages seen in the background. The teaser on the ad: "Crunchers of the Midway."

The two-page color-painting advertising spread in the center of the media guide promoted Heileman's Old Style beer.

At his farewell press conference, Ditka choked up but handled the sad moment with restraint. "I'll try to do this with class," Ditka said. "Scripture tells you that all things shall pass. This, too, shall pass."

It did. Ditka went on to coach the New Orleans Saints, then settled in Chicago, where he opened a popular restaurant with his name on it, delved into sports broadcasting, and made a living being Mike Ditka. He was always in demand for speeches, to write books, and for charity outings. He is revered in the City of Big Shoulders as a man with big shoulders who brought the town its Super Bowl title. Even if he didn't own his own restaurant, Ditka could dine off that accomplishment forever.

Sweetness

In the end, none of his usual protectors could run interference, and Walter Payton died young, waiting on a liver transplant list. His nickname was "Sweetness," yet Payton was a far tougher football player than most running backs. He was only 5'11" and 205 pounds, but he blocked like a lineman. He ran as much with balance and grit as he did with speed. And when he retired, he had run for more yards than Jim Brown, O. J. Simpson, Franco Harris—more than any of the elusive and powerful backs who made history and ran to glory.

"He was obviously the best," said onetime Bears fullback Matt Suhey, who shared the backfield with Payton when the Bears won the Super Bowl in 1986. "He's one of the all-time greats. He was a tremendously conditioned athlete, with great competitive spirit. Just an unbelievable amount, to take the pain and play through some very, very difficult times. Physically, anybody who can carry the ball and play that many games, that many years, how he did it, looking back I understand how good this guy was."

Payton starred at Jackson State in Mississippi, where he grew up, and he completed his bachelor's degree in three-and-a-half years before joining the Bears in 1975 as their number one draft pick. He held down the halfback slot through the 1987 season and rushed for an astronomical 16,726 yards at 4.4 yards per carry, while scoring 110 touchdowns on the ground and 125 in all. Besides the final totals in the major categories, Payton holds the team record for most attempts lifetime, in a season, and in a game. He rushed for 1,852 yards in 1977 and ten times topped the 1,000-yard mark in a season. When he rushed for 275 yards against Minnesota on November 20, 1977, it was an NFL record. He was chosen for the Pro Bowl nine times.

On occasion, the classy Payton was almost ridiculously self-effacing. In a 1985 game, when he rushed for 192 yards and the winning touchdown in a 16–10 victory over the Packers, Payton said, "Anybody could have done it. The offensive line blew open big holes." But of course, Payton, not just anybody, had done it.

He stressed that he wasn't the star of the game, but he was. He said the team was the star, which was true, but if so, he was the North Star that the other players followed.

Jay Hilgenberg, the longtime Chicago center out of Iowa, remembers the first play he tried to block for Payton in 1981. It didn't turn out the way the X and O charts said it would. Hilgen-

Sweet Career Highlights

Total yards (all purpose)—21,803
Rushing attempts, career—4,368
Rushing yards, career—16,726
Touchdowns—125
Touchdowns (season)—16 in 1977 and 1979
Points—750
100-yard rushing games (career)—77
100-yard rushing games (season) — 10 in 1977 and 1985

berg hit the ground after a block, and then bounced up ready to lead more interference for Payton, though he had spun around facing the other way.

"Right in front of me, all I could see was Walter Payton, and you know he had that long stride every now and then when he'd put his foot up in the air," Hilgenberg said. "He's coming, and he's doing that right in front of me. I'm trying to get out of the way, and I just caught his knee on my shoulder, and he went down. I think, on my first play, I'm tackling Walter Payton."

Payton looked at Hilgenberg and said, "'Hey, next time, just stay on the ground.' I knew my role."

From a distance, Payton seemed to be as sacred an icon as a priest, but those who knew him best understood he was no choirboy. He had a high-pitched laugh, and he giggled incessantly at his own practical jokes. Payton was as much prankster as power runner. He had a special sense for finding holes in the defensive line and for finding a teammate's weakness in a funny bone.

Coach Mike Ditka said that if there was an explosion or fire-works being set off, he knew Payton was behind it, and just because he was the coach he was not off limits. In one of his books, Ditka relays the story of how he'd receive phone calls at night when he was working late in his office from a Latino woman with a high-pitched voice. The woman said, "Meester Ditka, I am Yolanda. I want to meet you at the hotel down the street. I'm waiting for you. Please come, señor." The phone kept ringing for a month, and eventually Ditka discovered that Payton was the caller.

One reason defensive players respected Payton was that he seemed like one of them, had the same type of mentality. Some running backs scoot out of bounds to duck hits. They figure when they are cornered they are saving their bodies to run another day. However, Payton relished the contact. He wanted to hit defenders as badly as they wanted to hit him, sometimes even with his head down.

"Walter never ran out of bounds," said Bears former safety Gary Fencik. "He'd have three people who could really lick him, and he just wasn't going to step out of bounds and avoid the hit. As a defensive player you really got the opportunity to hit Walter. Occasionally during summer practice you kind of came into the

The great Walter Payton—running back, pass catcher, and blocker extraordinaire—could score touchdowns any which way, including flying high. *Chicago Tribune Archives*

hole, and you hit him harder than you probably should have. And Walter would look at you because you caught him by surprise a little bit. I'd go back to the huddle, strap it up, and he'd yell that the next time he sees me, he's going to really deliver a blow. Oh, God, he was awesome with the straight arm.

"He'd just run over you. Walter had that ability to deliver the blow, kind of get a stalemate out of a defender, and keep on running. It's the second effort you see with him time and time again on highlight films."

There is no such thing as a Bears highlight film without Walter Payton. He was the leading offensive force on the Super Bowl champions. And late in his career, his exploits were pivotal to making the Bears consistent winners. When he retired at the end of the 1987 season, Payton addressed a crowd of 62,000-plus at Soldier Field.

"I did it because it was fun," he said of his playing career. During the ceremonies, then mayor Eugene Sawyer awarded Payton the Chicago Medal of Merit. Payton, who had been honored as the NFL's man of the year in 1977, ultimately had the award named after him. The Bears retired his number 34 jersey. Payton, who had once been pulled over for driving 94 miles per hour on the street, dabbled in race-car driving. He also hoped to one day run his own expansion franchise.

Payton was elected to the Hall of Fame in 1993, and not surprisingly, he was not any more boastful upon learning of the honor than he had been when he was a star on the field. His first reaction to the news? "I'm embarrassed," Payton said. "Thrilled but embarrassed."

Embarrassed? If Payton had not been elected as soon as he

became eligible, the National Football League would have been embarrassed. Payton said he only played a kid's game, got paid for doing so, and enjoyed every minute of it. Those who watched him play knew that instinctively, just from the way he ran.

Payton, one of the most popular Chicago athletes of all time, retreated somewhat from the limelight after his retirement, but in early February of 1999 Payton held a stunning news conference. Looking somewhat shrunken and aged, he announced that he was afflicted with a rare liver disease called primary sclerosing cholangitis. Payton said he would need a liver transplant. And he revealed his deepest emotions.

"Hell, yeah, I'm scared," Payton said.

At the time, doctors indicated that Payton might live two more years without the transplant but also said that if a good match was found and surgery was successful, he could live many years and be as active as most people.

At the time, Payton had lost thirty-five pounds in four months. The key effect on his liver from the disease was narrowing of the bile duct because of inflammation and scarring. In the ensuing weeks Payton underwent additional testing at the Mayo Clinic and reported not doing very well while simultaneously predicting he would be OK. In the first few weeks following the announcement of his illness, Payton received an estimated 25,000 letters and cards wishing him well.

But from the first tentatively optimistic press conference on, Payton deteriorated. Cancer invaded his bile duct and made a transplant impractical. On November 1, about nine months later, Payton died at age forty-five. The death caught the city, and even many of his old teammates, by surprise.

Near the end of his life, Payton spent time with Suhey, who drove him on short trips and whom he continued to play light-hearted jokes on, and linebacker Mike Singletary, a religious player whom he prayed with. When news of Payton's death was publicized, one of Mike Ditka's first comments was that Payton was "the greatest Bear of them all." At Halas Hall, the Bears headquarters building, the American flag was lowered to half-staff.

It seemed impossible, unreal, that such a sturdy football hero, emblematic of probably the greatest Chicago Bears team, could be weakened and taken at such a young age. Despite the warning of Payton's illness, friends, fans, and former players found it difficult to believe that he was gone. Ditka said Payton felt he would obtain a liver transplant and resume a normal life, and Ditka believed it, too. So did many others.

As much as Payton was loved in Chicago, he occasionally recoiled from a goody-goody image and once said, "I'm not a role model. I'm just Walter Payton. If kids see some good in me they can utilize and emulate and make their lives better, so well and so good. But they have to realize I'm human just like anybody else. I'm capable of making mistakes. Nobody's perfect. Don't put that on me, because I'm not perfect."

Several days after his death, a ninety-minute memorial service was conducted for Payton at Soldier Field. About 15,000 people attended, many wearing their orange and blue Bears colors. "The light called Sweetness belongs to the heavens," the Reverend Jesse Jackson said. "Thank God for Sweetness."

Witnessing the tribute were Payton's wife, Connie; his children, including son Jarrett, who later played running back at the

Rushing for 1,000

Since the Chicago Bears were founded in 1920, the franchise has fielded only ten different running backs who rushed for 1,000 or more yards in a season. Walter Payton did it ten times, and Neal Anderson did it three times. Gale Sayers and Anthony Thomas are the only others to rush for that milestone number more than once.

Beattie Feathers's season might be the most remarkable. Not only was he ahead of his time (the Bears' next 1,000-yard runner did not appear for twenty-two years), he was injured and missed several games. His 8.4 yards per carry remains an all-time NFL record.

1934	Beattie Feathers	1,004
1956	Rick Casares	1,126
1966	Gale Sayers	1,231
1969	Gale Sayers	1,032
1976	Walter Payton	1,390
1977	Walter Payton	1,852
1978	Walter Payton	1,395
1979	Walter Payton	1,610
1980	Walter Payton	1,460
1981	Walter Payton	1,222
1983	Walter Payton	1,421
1984	Walter Payton	1,684
1985	Walter Payton	1,551
1986	Walter Payton	1,333
1988	Neal Anderson	1,106
1989	Neal Anderson	1,275
1990	Neal Anderson	1,078
1995	Rashaan Salaam	1,074
1997	Raymont Harris	1,033
2000	James Allen	1,120
2001	Anthony Thomas	1,183
2003	Anthony Thomas	1,024
2005	Thomas Jones	1,335

With a winning smile and a mischievous personality, Walter Payton made the Bears—and the NFL—a much better place to be. Chicago Tribune Archives

University of Miami and had been his father's presenter at the Hall of Fame in Canton, Ohio, as a twelve-year-old; and Payton's brother Eddie, another former NFL player. Members of the 1999 Bears team came as a group, and as they left the building, each player left a single rose next to a Payton poster. Posthumously, a book called *Never Die Easy* that Payton coauthored with writer Don Yaeger was released detailing Payton's struggle at the end of his life.

Walter Payton occupies a special place in the hearts of Chicago Bears fans, as well as in the minds of his teammates. They traveled long, difficult, and exhilarating roads together, and no one achieved more in the game than Sweetness.

During the 2005 football season, on a day the Bears met the Baltimore Ravens in a heavy rain, many members of the Super Bowl champs participated in a reunion event at Soldier Field. After players were introduced, defensive end Dan Hampton took the microphone and addressed the crowd.

"We were led by the greatest football player of all time," Hampton said to wild applause. "God bless Walter Payton."

Lean and Magical Years

It was a most unlikely addition to the Chicago Bears' wardrobe. On the last day of the regular season, when the Bears were officially anointed champions of the NFC Central Division with a 33–13 victory over the Jacksonville Jaguars, the T-shirts appeared as if by magic. Perhaps a sleight-of-hand magician fed scarves into his secret box and transformed them into souvenirs capping the unexpected 2001 season.

Linebacker Warrick Holdman gazed at the new top hanging in his locker and calculated what to do with it. "I'll probably wear it for a week," he said. "Then I'll frame it."

The years between the 1986 Super Bowl championship and the 2001 Bears turned over generations of players and depressed generations of fans. From being kings of the world, the Bears had declined to commoners. They had gone from contenders to pretenders, from royalty to bad news Bears. In a town that loved them best of all its professional sports teams, the Bears had gone from providers of joy to suppliers of doom. They ranked right next to the next-beloved team, the baseball Cubs, for offering disappointment. Fans were beaten down, their optimism shelved, their cynicism rampant.

One exception, a success that will be everlasting in team lore, was the Bears' 20–12 victory over the Eagles in a 1988 playoff game in Chicago. The game is known as the Fog Bowl, because for the final thirty-two minutes of play a dense fog enveloped the stadium, and hardly anyone saw what happened. Neither TV announcers nor fans in the stands could see the field. Put it this way: Everyone thinks the Bears won.

Although the Bears did not repeat their Super Bowl journey, they finished 14–2 in the 1986 regular season, went 11–4 in 1987, and were 12–4 in 1988. Even now, many players of that era believe they should have won three Super Bowls. There was a one-year, 6–10 disaster in 1989, but the Bears rebounded to go 11–5 in both 1990 and 1991.

Except for a couple of 9–7 seasons tucked into the middle, the end of Mike Ditka's coaching reign and the follow-up regime of Dave Wannstedt accomplished little. In 2000 the Bears finished 5–11, and nobody saw 13–3 coming in 2001 under Dick Jauron. There were no clues that a breakout season awaited.

Even when the Bears began winning that autumn, the truest of fans were skeptical, loathe to give their hearts to a team that was sure to collapse, that was certain to lead them on and then crush their spirits. How could the Bears be back when they had a rookie running back, a defense with few big names, and a quarterback whom most fans had to look up on a scorecard?

But Anthony "A Train" Thomas, fresh out of Michigan, rushed for 1,183 yards, linebacker Brian Urlacher demonstrated that he was the latest great at a position rich in Bears tradition, and quarterback Jim Miller showed he could get the job done, especially with end Marty Booker making 100 catches.

After predictably opening with a loss to the defending Super Bowl champion Baltimore Ravens, the Bears stifled the intradivision rival Minnesota Vikings, 17–10. Always satisfying. And then Chicago swept past Atlanta 31–3 on the road (whoa!). Next came wins over Arizona, Cincinnati (Thomas rushed for 188 yards), San Francisco, and Cleveland—the latter two in overtime at Soldier Field, both on touchdown returns via interceptions by free safety Mike Brown.

In both instances, comebacks looked hopeless and fans were exiting. In both sequences, Brown stunned witnesses with magnificent plays that rank among the flashiest in team history. He taught spectators never to leave their seats before the final gun.

The 49ers led 31–16 midway through the fourth quarter, and after the 37–31 final-result calamity, quarterback Jeff Garcia could only say he was "in shock." It was a one-in-a-million play for Brown, a spectacular 33-yard interception for a TD akin to hitting a home run with two outs in the bottom of the tenth inning.

And then he did the exact same thing a week later, giving the Bears a 27–21 victory over the Browns. Even more remarkably, the Bears trailed 21–7 with less than a minute remaining in regulation. Shane Matthews was in at quarterback for the injured Miller. Matthews hit Booker for a touchdown pass. Then the Bears recovered an onside kick, and in the last second Matthews found running back James Allen in the end zone for the tying score. The play was the dictionary definition of a Hail Mary pass. In overtime, defensive end Bryan Robinson batted a Browns pass into the air, and Brown picked it off and ran it in for the clinching touchdown. Brown had performed an instant replay on a once-a-career savior play.

Teams often complain about a lack of respect, but after being down for so long, it was a genuine gripe for the Bears. Their own fans were slow to embrace them as being for real. Sports broadcasters and sports columnists took a wait-and-see outlook. Nationwide, football fans were hesitant to declare them a true threat. And the players understood it every step of the way. They huddled in their locker room and at their practices, blocking out distractions and dissenters. And they completed the regular-season task as division champs for the first time in eleven years.

The Bears were winning, bringing back old-time, feel-good memories. Whenever the Bears are on a roll during the cold-weather months, it warms the town. "This feels great," Bryan Robinson said. "To prove everybody wrong is the biggest thing."

It was no accident that the Bears' main strength that season was the defense. Whenever Chicago posts an outstanding record, you can be fairly certain that the Monsters of the Midway ties are strong. It was true in 1963, and it was true in 1985. In 2001, the Bears allowed just 203 points.

Following a sterling rookie year, Urlacher was building a reputation as one of the NFL's best defensive players. He notched 148 tackles during the 2001 season, 92 of them solo, collected 3 interceptions and 8 sacks. It wasn't long before he emerged as the most popular pro athlete in the city.

A few years later, the 6'4", 258-pound defensive leader who played collegiate ball at New Mexico, repeatedly returned to 2001 memories to recall some of his favorite football moments.

"It was unbelievable," said Urlacher, remembering the entire season for being as filled with magic as Harry Potter's school. "We did what we had to do to win every game. We went down and we pounded Atlanta. We shut out Cincinnati. We beat Tampa Bay twice. We played well. It was a neat season."

Before injuries, trades, and free agency broke it up, that defense had the makings of a unit worthy of its own nickname, like Minnesota's old Purple People Eaters. Warrick Holdman and Roosevelt Colvin flanked Urlacher at linebacker. The front four was Phillip Daniels, Keith Traylor, Ted Washington, and Bryan Robinson. The defensive backfield featured Mike Brown, Tony Parrish, Walt Harris, and R. W. McQuarters. The squad recorded two shutouts and held five teams to 6 points or less.

"For thirteen games we played great on defense," Urlacher said. "The camaraderie we had that year was unbelievable. We had pretty much the same starters all year, and we got along. We had fun out there. Even in practice we had fun."

Urlacher is one player who believes that being tight with teammates is important, that a bickering team is not a winning

Brian Urlacher quickly became the heart and soul of the Bears' twenty-first-century defense. Chicago Tribune Archives

team. The whole is more important than the sum of parts. "If you don't get along with your teammates, it's not that it's hard to win, but it's a lot more fun when you get along and you do stuff together and hang out," Urlacher said. "It's hard to get along with someone as much time as we spend. We're together every day. During training camp it's fifteen hours. We work out together every day. We meet together every day with our coaches, and it gets old, but if you like who you work with, you enjoy it."

When the Philadelphia Eagles trounced the Bears, 33–19, at Soldier Field in the playoffs, it was anticlimactic. Yet the fans basked in the season's accomplishments and the record of a team that offered promise for the next season.

And then in 2002 the Bears drove off a cliff, finishing a dismal 4–12. It made the 2001 season seem like a mirage. Dick Jauron had earned himself some good will and a new contract and bought some time. But when the Bears finished 7–9 in 2003, general manager Jerry Angelo was out of patience. Jauron was fired, and Angelo hitched his wagon to Lovie Smith, the defensive coordinator of the St. Louis Rams. The Bears were starting over. Again.

Life with Lovie began with the 2004 season, and in many ways it differed little from some of the lowest points in the recent decade. The Bears finished 5–11. The Bears had no established quarterback. The defense was stingy, and the offense was ineffective.

The awkward history of Bears quarterbacking was acted out with a new-millennium version of an old stage play. Chicago had drafted Rex Grossman out of the University of Florida, with plans to mold him into the quarterback of the future. He was handed the keys to the kingdom but after a few games was injured and knocked out for the year. So as the defense did its darnedest to knock the snot out of opposing offenses, the Bears' anemic offense was shunted from Grossman to Chad Hutchinson to Jonathan Quinn to Craig Krenzel. Each game was suspenseful (when was the next interception or fumble coming?) and demoralizing to watch.

It seemed impossible for a professional football team to line up so many different characters at the most important position on the field who seemed to have as little chance to move the team forward as a Pop Warner kid. The fodder for sports talk radio was nutritious. When the team staggered to the finish line, the primary topic was just how great things would be when Grossman returned and continued his development into the next Joe Montana.

And then along came training camp, the summer of 2005, and Grossman was injured again. Remarkably, for the second straight year, Angelo had not signed a veteran backup. The situation screamed out for emergency assistance. Instead, the Bears gave the job to Hutchinson. Bears fans groaned, anticipating another dreary season. But when Hutchinson struck out this time, Angelo acted swiftly. He signed seasoned vet Jeff Blake and banished Hutchinson to the waiver wire. Then the Bears inserted fourth-round draft pick Kyle Orton as the starter.

Orton figured to be a long-term project. He had done exceptional work at Purdue, though he was held back by injury his senior year. Neither he nor Smith nor Grossman expected to see the 6'4", 223-pound former Big Ten star calling plays as a rookie, unless it was on the scout team. Orton, however, was a natural leader who seemed to have the goods, if not the experience.

The circumstances of Grossman's injury and Orton's ascension offered little comfort to the average team observer. Didn't rookie quarterbacks get devoured by hungry defensive linemen and become wolfpack prey to marauding sack seekers?

The Bears started slowly, going 1–3 in their first four games. Long winter, people felt. When's Grossman coming back? they asked. Only a funny thing happened. Orton did not tear up defenses with huge plays, but he displayed the demeanor of a ten-year veteran. He was the boss in the huddle, and he made the necessary plays to win. At the same time a new generation of defenders rekindled the links to the Monsters of the Midway. Or at least brought to mind the exploits of Dan "Danimal" Hampton and Steve "Mongo" McMichael from the 1985 wild bunch.

Urlacher was the cornerstone, but defensive end Adewale Ogunleye was the sack master. The Bears ran the ball behind gutsy, steady Thomas Jones, and Orton found end Muhsin Muhammad downfield. The defense at first controlled foes and then gradually began to dominate them. After the slow start, the Bears won five games in a row to move to 6–3 and take over a comfortable lead in the NFC North Division ahead of the Vikings, Lions, and Packers. The Bears were in first place. First place. They liked the sound of that phrase. Much like 2001, it was also hard to believe that the team was for real, that it wasn't a house of cards.

Just as in that bolt-from-the-blue season, the 2005 campaign unfolded with a sense of unreality. At first, fans didn't attach any meaning to the victories. By the tenth game of the season, when the Carolina Panthers were due at Soldier Field, the matchup was being described as a barometer of the whole year. The Bears had beaten only weak teams? Fine. The Panthers came to Chicago touted as a preseason National Football Conference

The Rebuilding of the Bears

When the Bears began to win again during the 2005 season, the roster was loaded with players who had been drafted in 2004 and 2005 under the guidance of general manager Jerry Angelo and new coach Lovie Smith.

2004	No. 1	Defensive tackle	Tommie Harris
	No. 2	Defensive tackle	Tank Johnson
	No. 3	Wide receiver	Bernard Berrian
	No. 4a	Cornerback	Nathan Vasher
	No. 4b	Linebacker	Leon Joe
	No. 5b	Quarterback	Craig Krenzel
2005	No. 1	Running back	Cedric Benson
	No. 2	Wide receiver	Mark Bradley
	No. 4	Quarterback	Kyle Orton
	No. 5	Wide receiver	Airese Currie
	No. 6	Safety	Chris Harris

favorite to reach the Super Bowl. The Panthers came to Chicago with a 7–2 record. The Panthers came to Chicago with an offense that had more of a kick than moonshine, averaging 27.7 points per game. OK, bring them on.

The stakes were hardly as meaningful, but the 2005 Bears defense did to the Panthers what the 1985 Bears did to the Patriots in the Super Bowl. They intimidated and humiliated. They terrorized and vaporized. Chicago won, 13–3, and the Panthers were bent, folded, and mutilated. From the first quarter on, the Bears pulverized the Panthers.

Nathan Vasher, an emerging sensation at cornerback in his second season out of the University of Texas, ruined Carolina in the first half. The week before, as the Bears topped the San Francisco 49ers, Vasher lunged to catch a missed field-goal attempt and then ran it back 108 yards for a touchdown, the longest return in NFL history.

Against Carolina, Vasher added to his budding status as a playmaker by intercepting two Jake Dellhomme passes in the early going. Dellhomme threw poorly to the left side; Vasher cradled the ball and returned it 46 yards to the Panther 8 yard line. That set up the Bears for an easy touchdown. Dellhomme apparently couldn't resist trying to show that his first call was the right one and threw another pass to the same zone, again to Vasher rather than to a Panther. This time Vasher ran the ball back 22 yards, and the Bears collected a field goal for a 10–0 lead that was good enough to last. The Panthers wilted, and by game's end, the Bears had notched eight sacks, including three by Ogunleye.

Panthers guard Tutan Reyes was one of the linemen turned into a sieve. "They are the number one defense for a reason," Reyes said.

At 5'10" and 180 pounds, Vasher was just about the smallest player on the defense, but he kept making the biggest plays. "I make them all look easy," Vasher joked.

The win put the Bears on the map again and made the rest of the league and the country take notice. Lovie Smith was making the bad news vanish. The Bears of the present had morphed into the Bears of the future and reestablished ties to the glorious past.

Being a Bear

The song is played at every home game. The words appear on an electronic, circular message board at Soldier Field. The Bears have a fight song that dates to 1941, and while it isn't the catchiest of tunes, it does have staying power.

"Bear Down, Chicago Bears" is a pretty hokey song, almost like an alma mater at a state university whose students revel in its sheer campiness when singing. It sounds as if it is from a bygone era, even older than its dated creation.

Bears in the Hall

The Pro Football Hall of Fame opened in Canton, Ohio, in 1963, and the oldest franchise has the most players enshrined. The Bears claim twenty-six members of the Hall, even if some of those players developed some of their sterling credentials elsewhere. The Bears represent all eras of the game.

Of course, first on the list, the first Bear inducted in the charter class, was George Halas, Papa Bear, Mr. NFL, whose involvement with the league spanned sixty-three years. Halas was notable as a player, coach, owner, and contributor. No one did more for the league in its first six decades of existence. Here are the other Bears enshrined in the Hall of Fame:

Doug Atkins	Defensive end
George Blanda	Quarterback-kicker
Dick Butkus	Linebacker
George Connor	Tackle-linebacker
Mike Ditka	Tight end
John "Paddy" Driscoll	Running back

The songwriting credit goes to Jerry Downs, a pseudonym for Al Hoffman, a songwriter who was better known for writing the tune "If I Knew You Were Coming, I'd Have Baked a Cake." Perhaps that would have worked for the Bears, also, if it were played each time they knocked on the end zone door. In any case, Mr. Downs/Hoffman would probably be surprised that his

Jim Finks	General manager
Danny Fortmann	Guard
Bill George	Linebacker
Harold "Red" Grange	Running back–defensive back
Dan Hampton	Defensive end
Ed Healey	Tackle
Bill Hewitt	End
Stan Jones	Tackle–guard–defensive tackle
Sid Luckman	Quarterback
Roy "Link" Lyman	Tackle
George McAfee	Running back–defensive back
George Musso	Tackle–guard–defensive tackle
Bronko Nagurski	Tackle-fullback
Walter Payton	Running back
Gale Sayers	Running back
Mike Singletary	Linebacker
Joe Stydahar	Tackle
George Trafton	Center
Clyde "Bulldog" Turner	Center-linebacker

football song still gets airtime more than sixty-five years after he penned it.

While never is heard a praising word from a player saying that the song inspired him to make a long touchdown run, the quaint tradition of urging patrons at Soldier Field to sing along seems appropriate for the oldest franchise in the National Football League. It is just old-timey enough to make fans think of the leather helmet era.

One thing Bears do honor and appreciate is the history that surrounds the team. Bears fans are proud that their team has been around since 1920, and they exult in the fact that their team has won so many championships. Bears fans, true Chicagoans who grew up in the neighborhoods, identify with the Bears on a different level—they are not just a sports team. The Bears are part of the city's identity, representatives of residents who shovel out their parking spaces in front of their houses and then claim them for the winter with old chairs, of those who work the long shifts doing work that leaves calluses on their hands, and of those who feel that the Bears are part of the fabric of their city.

The Green Bay Packers are owned by the community, a unique trait. The New York Giants have longevity but are rarely as glitzy as Madison Avenue would have them be. In the case of the Bears, founded by a gruff, hard-driving coach who presided over decades of stability and success, and Chicago, the capital of the Midwest, the community that rewards hard work more than slickness, the match is perfect. Chicago and the Bears fit together. The players who come to town from other parts of the nation soon recognize the rare linkage that differs from other cities in the league. In Chicago, there is always precedent, there is always someone to compare yourself against.

Red Grange begat Gale Sayers who begat Walter Payton. Bill George begat Dick Butkus who begat Mike Singletary who begat Brian Urlacher. The 1934 championship team begat the 1963 championship team, which begat the Super Bowl XX champions. The Monsters of the Midway begat the 1963 defense, which begat the 1980s defense, which begat the 2001 defense, which begat the 2005 defense. In Chicago, the Bears live with ghosts of greats as much as they do with the current weekly schedule.

For decades George Halas told the newcomers what it meant to be a Bear. Or rather he taught them. You were supposed to outwork the other guy, give your all, and hit as hard as Bronko Nagurski and Clyde "Bulldog" Turner. It was your responsibility to live up to the tradition established in the 1920s and nurtured ever since.

The Bears and the community reflect each other's qualities almost mirrorlike in the clear waters of Lake Michigan. Part of Mike Ditka's genius—why he was the right coach at the right time for the Bears and why Halas selected Ditka—was his natural understanding of the connection. Ditka played up the image of the mid-1980s Bears as a group of guys who punched in, did their job, and were not afraid to get dirt under their fingernails. It is no mean feat getting the average Joe who really does work on an assembly line or digs ditches to identify with a rich professional athlete, but Ditka performed the trick.

"They can identify with us," lineman Keith Van Horne said years later of Bears fans in a working-class town. "You get the blue-collar and the white-collar fan, but I think, as Ditka put it so beautifully, 'We're a bunch of Grabowskis.' And I think that's how we're looked at and appreciated. It's just hard-nosed, three-yards-and-a-cloud-of-dust football. Maybe that football isn't going to win so many games for you anymore—obviously the game's changed—but that's sort of how people look at it."

Actually, with their throwback defense and their hesitation to throw a rookie quarterback into the furnace, the 2005 Bears won with precisely the old-school format of defense and a running game.

"There's also just the history," Van Horne said, "the fact that George Halas started the NFL. The history is there, and I think the city of Chicago takes great pride in that."

Clearly, there is something deeper than simple fandom at work in the manner that Bears rooters stick with their team during bad times as well as good. It is openly acknowledged that in a city that boasts two Major League Baseball teams; one of the original six National Hockey League teams; and a professional basketball team that won six world titles led by Michael Jordan, the most exciting player of all time, that the Bears are still tops, the Bears are first among equals, the Bears are the favorite child.

Emory Moorehead, the mid-1980s tight end who played on the Super Bowl championship squad, grew up in Evanston, just north of Chicago, and settled in the suburbs after his playing career. He has been a Chicago sports fan his whole life, and although he may be biased because he played for the Bears, he thinks the area just adores the team.

"You know, at any time, they love the Bears," Moorehead said. "This town, they won six world championships with the Bulls. But if you give the Bears a division championship, that means more than six world championships. Because the Bears go back. They go back generations and generations with families following the Bears. The image of Chicago is the Bears."

Willie Gault, the speedster who was a spectacular receiver during the Super Bowl era, is a Hollywood guy now, an actor, but he sounds nostalgic when he talks about the way the Bears and Chicago bonded.

"It was perfect," Gault said of the Super Bowl titlists. "Chicago was always the second city in everything, but we notched a couple of firsts. By the Bears winning the Super Bowl, it actually changed the city's mindset and made us and the city of Chicago number one across the nation. Not second to New York or Los Angeles. Chicago had a workmanlike attitude and atmosphere, and that's exactly what the Bears were. We went out hard and played hard, and we got results from that."

When the Super Bowl defenders were in their heyday, the leading tackler was frequently safety Gary Fencik, whom Ditka called "the brains of our defense." Fencik thinks a key reason for the connection between the Bears and Chicago is defense. It may just be that Chicago is more of a brick wall town than a pretty, long-bomb town. Joe Namath was made for Broadway and New York. The snarling middle linebackers were made for Chicago.

The old Jets might figure if Joe had a good day, the team would have a good day. Fencik said the Bears read things differently.

"When you get in a huddle, you can listen to the defensive line," Fencik said. "It gives you a pretty good sense really of whether or not they're going to have a good day, And if your defensive line has a good day, everybody else is going to be having a good day, as well."

A different barometer for sure. Some players in certain sports say they step to the plate, they dribble downcourt, without ever hearing the crowd's cheers. In a big, jam-packed, 60,000-person football stadium, teams soak up the noise. They know a home crowd can disrupt a visiting quarterback's play calling. Frequently, observers will see defenders waving their arms, boosting the crowd, making windmill motions for more, more, more.

Longtime Bears center Jay Hilgenberg fed on crowd noise. He even felt the same ripples of goose bumps as a spectator at other Chicago sporting events. The Chicago Blackhawks have long punctuated the scoring of a goal with a deep-bassed horn that sounds like a freighter coming at the net.

"I used to love to go to the Blackhawks at the old stadium," Hilgenberg said of the long-gone Chicago Stadium. "That fired you up, being an athlete. You want to perform at a high level in an atmosphere like that. That's what you work hard for, I guess. The whole thing was unbelievable."

It is often said that modern-day athletes have no sense of history, that the only history they are aware of concerning their sport and their team is what they happened to see on ESPN *Sports Center* the night before. That may be why it took a speech from Mike Ditka to inform young players that others came before them blazing a trail, that other teams wearing the same uniform preceded them and accomplished glorious things.

If team sports are about sharing with everyone who is on that field wearing the same uniform, then in the right organization, with the proper history lesson, it can also be about honoring those who wore the same uniform before you were born.

One player who got it was Tim Wrightman, a former Bears tight end, who now lives in Idaho and operates a hunting lodge. It was not as if Wrightman behaved like a little kid haunting hotel lobbies to obtain autographs of famous Bears, but he took advantage of his position, because of his respect for the team's history, to collect tangible evidence of his Bears ties.

In the mid-1980s, Wrightman attended a banquet in California honoring the college players selected for the Walter Camp

All-America team. One of the guests of honor was Red Grange. "Great guy," Wrightman said. "He signed an autograph for me."

On the plane heading to road trips during his two seasons with the Bears, Wrightman sometimes sat with team chairman Ed McCaskey and listened to him tell stories about Bears of the past. "I said, 'You know, I would love to have an autographed picture from Bronko Nagurski, if he's still alive,'" Wrightman requested once. "And Ed said at the time, 'Yeah, he's in his 80s, but he lives in Duluth, Minnesota, and I talk to his son all the time.' I said, 'If it ever could happen, I'd love it.'"

Three weeks later, Wrightman received an autographed picture from Bronko Nagurski, and it hangs on the wall in his home. Wrightman refers to one room in his lodge as his "Bear Den." Among the decorations are autographs of Grange, Nagurski, Walter Payton, Gale Sayers, and Sid Luckman. "I have the four greatest running backs in Chicago Bears history in that room," Wrightman said.

He does not own an autographed picture of George Halas, who died just as Wrightman was joining the team. Wrightman grew up in California and attended UCLA and said he did not follow pro football as a kid. He had no idea who Papa Bear Halas was until much later. Wrightman doesn't have Halas on his wall of fame, but he does have Halas's signature on the "Welcome to the Bears" letter the team owner wrote to him after the Bears drafted him in the third round in 1982.

"I got to meet him when the Bears drafted me," Wrightman said. "The next day they flew me to Chicago for a press conference. Then he died. I never met him again."

Chicagoans have long memories when the topic is the Bears.

Supernova Instead of Super Bowl

It was the type of locker room where the loudest sound was the slow drip from a shower. Like any other athletes, Bears players thought they would win. Like any other football players, Bears players thought they were bound for the Super Bowl.

Instead, the 2005 season of great promise ended a game shy of the National Football Conference championship game, ended before any kind of playoff run was mounted. After winning the NFC North Division and earning a first-round bye with their 11–5 record, the Bears went bye-bye, falling to the Carolina Panthers, 29–21, at Soldier Field.

They were shocked because they beat Carolina during the regular season. They were shocked because it was a home game. And they were shocked because their potent defense surrendered 434 yards.

"You know, obviously we're all extremely disappointed," quarterback Rex Grossman said. "We all didn't play the game that we practiced all week and got ready for. But what can I say? I'm going to be ready to go next year, and our whole team is. We're really mad in here, but also we're still hungry."

In the giddiness of the lead-up to the playoff game, it was forgotten just how far the Bears had traveled. In preseason, no one expected eleven wins. No one expected a division championship. No one expected to make the playoffs.

What 2005 showed is that the Bears were back. The Monsters of the Midway seemed set to roar again.

Once a Bear, always a Bear in the public's eyes. Once a Super Bowl Bear, always a sainted Bear in the public's eyes.

Moorehead works in banking, and barely a day goes by, especially during the football season, when his Bears connection is not mentioned. He is amazed how often the 1985 season comes up in conversation—and not only with guys. He is constantly surprised at the number of women who talk about how the colorful Super Bowl team with Mongo, The Fridge, and Payton snared their interest.

"I've had a lot of women say, 'My husband is crazy about the Bears, but in 1985 I started watching, and I learned about football from you guys,'" Moorehead said. "So the team got a whole other generation of Bears fans rekindled. The Bears are the team of this town. They're the number one thing—it's always been that way. The only thing that will ever come close is if the Cubs win the World Series. If the Cubs ever win, you're going to have people coming out all over the world claiming they were Cubs fans."

On the same day Moorehead spoke about Bears history, he had made a business call to the suburban Chicago community offices of the Village of Niles and was asked if he was *the* Emory Moorehead.

"People remember," Moorehead said. "They knew who you were before you won, but after you won, it's like they know you and want to be a part of you. They always identify you. Things aren't going to change. People love the Bears."

Moorehead talks about the Bears from the special perspective of rooting for team success as a youngster and then being part of its greatest success in recent decades as a participant.

"I grew up a Bears fan," Moorehead said. "I followed Gale Sayers and Dick Butkus and all those guys. So to get a chance to play for your hometown team was very special. But to win it all? I understood how it had been and how frustrating it had been. And I understood that if you win the Super Bowl here in Chicago, you're in here forever. You're in for life."

You gain membership in a special, tiny club where the singing voices of tens of thousands of supplicants ring in your ears.

About the Author

Lew Freedman is a sportswriter for the *Chicago Tribune*, where he has played a role in Bears coverage since 2001. Freedman has won numerous journalism awards and is the author of twenty-four books.

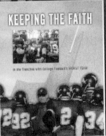
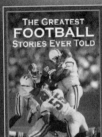